The Workers' Union

FLORA TRISTAN

The Workers' Union

Translated
with an introduction by
BEVERLY LIVINGSTON

University of Illinois Press
URBANA CHICAGO LONDON

First Illinois paperback, 2007
© 1983 by the Board of Trustees
of the University of Illinois
All rights reserved
Manufactured in the United States of America
P 5 4 3 2 1

The Library of Congress cataloged
the cloth edition of this volume as follows:

Tristan, Flora, 1803–1844.
The workers' union.
Translation of: Union ouvrière.
Bibliography: p.
Includes index.
1. Trade-unions—France—History.
2. Labor and laboring classes—France—History. I. Title.
HD6684.T6713   331.88'0944 82-1891

Paperback ISBN-13: 978-0-252-07529-2
Paperback ISBN-10: 0-252-07529-3

CONTENTS

TRANSLATOR'S INTRODUCTION

The Workers' Union, first published on June 1, 1843, was the last of Flora Tristan's writing to appear before her death in November 1844 at the age of forty-one. What she affectionately called her "little book" not only drew together various threads of her thinking but, more important, proposed a plan for real action. The circumstances surrounding the book's publication and dissemination revealed its progressive and controversial position. The time was both ripe and ill-prepared for the visionary project contained in Tristan's little book.

Flora Tristan thoroughly understood this contradiction about her times and placed it at the very core of her analysis. Focusing her discussion upon the workers' immobilization and deplorable degradation, she appealed to their need and desire for autonomy so that their conquest over ignorance through education and their rise from debasement by means of unification could begin. Worker unity, she argued, was the necessary condition for the creation of a Working Class, the sole effective means of improving the lot of France's "most numerous and useful class." Tristan did not restrict her argument to France alone; she was in fact the *first* to call for an international association of the proletariat, the "universal unionization" of workers.[1]

She was also among the first to insist that the condition of women deserved a central place in any program of working-class reform. From personal experience Tristan knew that women were economically disadvantaged and held back by their lack of edu-

1. Tristan, *The Workers' Union*, chap. IV, fn. 3. And also, G. D. H. Cole, *Socialist Thought*, vol. I (New York: St. Martin's Press, 1954), p. 188.

cation. Her most radical formulation equated women and the proletariat by describing both as society's "pariahs." The liberation of one, she maintained in an early statement of socialist-feminism, was inseparable from the liberation of the other.

The Woman

Who was the author of this remarkable text? Although she was not of working-class birth, the circumstances of Tristan's family led her to understand the plight of French workers. Flora Tristan was born in 1803, the daughter of Marie Thérèse Laisney, a French woman, and Don Mariano Tristan y Moscozo, a Peruvian aristocrat. She was never permitted, nor did she allow herself, to forget her paternal heritage. Pride and a certain exotic allure were part of the legacy passed on to her by her father, who died when she was four. But more problematic was her legal status, discovered after her father's death. Her parents' religious marriage in Spain had not been legitimized by the French authorities. As a result, the family had no judicial recourse to the property in the father's name: Flora was technically illegitimate. Devoid of any legal rights, she would later realize the full implication of her dilemma and would compare it to the disenfranchisement of the working class. At seventeen she learned the lithographic coloring trade.[2] When her employer, André Chazal, proposed marriage, she accepted. Within four years, Flora was pregnant for the third time; and, thoroughly alienated from a husband who continually brutalized her, she decided to abandon her home. Cast again into social marginality, Tristan was then confronted with her status as a triple pariah: the natural daughter of Don Mariano, deserter of the domestic hearth, and female in a society that did not recognize rights for women.

2. Some would like to consider the artistic talent as well as the penchant for the exotic of Tristan's grandson, Paul Gauguin, to be inherited from his maternal grandmother.

In her quest for independence and knowledge of the world, Tristan undertook various travels. Her early trips to England and possibly other points in Europe remain clouded and undocumented, in all likelihood because the humiliation she would have endured in the personal service of an English lady or family kept her from wanting to discuss them. They were, however, important opportunities for the discovery of other cultures, for developing techniques of observation later to be of immeasurable service.

Then, completely on her own, in April 1833 on the day of her thirtieth birthday, she embarked from Bordeaux on an arduous sea-journey. Her destination was Peru, her mission to request her share of the paternal inheritance. In a letter before her departure, she had cautiously hid the fact that she was married and the mother of three children, but made the fatal error of appealing to her uncle's generosity by mentioning the status of her parents' union. Her misfortune was compounded by her grandmother's death, which had occurred almost to the day she sailed from France. Some four months later, Flora arrived in Arequipa, to be warmly received as a member of the extended family and eventually invited to live on the estate. She was flatly refused anything substantial in her own right, however. Though emotionally tattered, Flora managed to take an active interest in political and social issues during her Peruvian sojourn, proving herself an astute witness, and even occasionally sought after for her commentary. During the eight or nine months she remained in South America, writing assumed a central role in her life, for her private journal was her only consolation. In it she vented her emotional distress and displayed fully her powers of critical observation. The diary resulted in her first major publication, a two-volume work, *Les Pérégrinations d'une paria* (1838), which anticipated the future development of her thinking. Her sympathetic yet penetrating look at South American women announced a feminist outlook that understood women in their socioeconomic context. And because of the instability she witnessed in the initial stage of

Peru's nationhood, Tristan also learned to judge the mechanics of power and the meaning of social values threatened by political gamesmanship.

Not long after her return to Paris in 1834, she began writing pamphlets addressing questions of social inequity. The first, "On the Necessity of Welcoming Foreign Women" (1836), followed directly from her experiences as a single woman traveling alone. The second pamphlet, dated December 20, 1837, for submission to the Chamber of Deputies, was her "Petition for the Reinstatement of Divorce." (Divorce had been granted in 1792, during the Revolution, but was abolished in 1816 by the Restoration government. It was not legalized again until 1884.) A year later her third and final pamphlet was submitted to the Chamber, a "Petition for the Abolition of Capital Punishment." Dated December 10, 1838, it reflects not only Tristan's fundamental humanitarian sentiment, but also her lack of vindictiveness, for just three months before she had been the victim of an attempted murder perpetrated by her estranged husband. The trial proceedings are the sole source of information about the tribulations and horrors she and her children suffered. They tell of her attempts to flee Chazal, who cruelly and violently sought to keep her from her children.[3]

Earlier in that eventful year of 1838, her book *Méphis* appeared, giving her a name as a novelist. Though she projected other fictional texts (for instance, *La Fille de Lima*), she never managed to write them. Her one work of fiction, while generally solidly structured, was not a felicitously written novel. Excessive tangential developments and typically Romantic conventions of exaggerated coincidences and melodramatic dialogue merely exacerbate a heavy didacticism which today's reader tends to find offensive.

But Tristan had other projects to pursue. Within two years of publishing her novel, she was appealing to workers to toss aside

3. *Gazette des Tribunaux*, February 1, 1839.

stories and fiction in favor of "serious" works, such as her own, elucidating the proletarian condition.[4] By this time she had obviously come into contact with various Utopian programs that were gaining popularity in Restoration France. Her novel *Méphis* shows strains of Saint-Simonism and Fourierist thinking, and it is known that she had the opportunity to meet the English socialist Robert Owen upon his visit to Paris in 1837.

In 1839 Tristan made her fourth and last trip to Great Britain. She undertook this final foreign voyage with the express intent of completing her observations on British life and society in the form of a series of reports or essays, *Promenades dans Londres* (1840). Edited four times in two years, the book is a precursor of Friedrich Engels's *The Condition of the English Working Class* (1845). In *Promenades*, Tristan's journalistic talent was fully exploited, and her feminist-socialist perspective fully tested. Nothing in Britain escaped her critical gaze: from the way upper-class mothers greet their children to how the countryside is parceled (enclosures), to a day at the races. With a strong narrative presence, the rhetorical mode of the *Promenades* might be described as exclamatory. The style underscores her compassion for the unfortunate, her outcry against bourgeois and aristocratic privilege, and her own peculiar brand of national chauvinism.

Soon after returning to Paris, Tristan decided to take the small and natural, yet courageous, leap from exclamatory rhetoric to the rhetoric of action. With her usual intensity she embarked on an ambitious program, initiated in the writing of *The Workers' Union* and pursued with assiduous effort. Her untimely death at forty-one cut short her mission to solidify the French working class. However, in the little time she had, Tristan managed to see or contact literally hundreds of individuals who supported her quest to unify the workers' and women's causes.

4. "Dedication to the French Workers," *Promenades dans Londres* (Paris, 1842).

The Times

The first important date in French proletarian history, 1831, fell, significantly, during Tristan's formative period.[5] This was the year of worker rioting in Lyons following a general wage decrease (in 1830) and resulting in a government ban on workers' associations. More specifically, the employers' refusal to set a minimum wage for textile workers (October 1831) served as a catalyst fomenting proletarian resentment and unrest which, in December, finally erupted into full-scale rioting necessitating the intervention of the national guard. The Lyons uprising was especially meaningful because it signaled the advent of a "new" potential force, that of the proletariat.[6]

As in Britain, the development of industrial capitalism led to deteriorating conditions for French workers. Fourteen- and sixteen-hour work days were not uncommon. Wages were often well below the subsistence level (women received half the wages men did, children even less). The primary locations of working-class resistance to proletarianization during the early 1830s were Paris and Lyons, where the largest concentrations of skilled workers lived. The French economy was still primarily dominated by artisanal organizations, unlike that of Britain, whose industrialization had advanced more rapidly. Existent since the Middle Ages, artisanal fraternities called "compagnonnages" attempted to come to the aid of their members. These secret associations offered both financial and emotional assistance, but were also rife with abuses and were viciously pitted one against the other. Their most serious drawback, and the aspect quickly grasped by Tristan, was their incapacity, as an institution, to lead or even contribute significantly to a general labor movement in the name of the whole working class. She understood that these groups con-

5. According to Paul Louis, the other two salient proletarian moments in French history fall in 1848 and 1871; see Louis, *Histoire du socialisme en France* (Paris: Marcel Rivière, 1950), p. 102.

6. *Ibid.*, p. 95.

stituted a kind of proletarian "aristocracy" to which unskilled laborers and women could never aspire and whose continuation would only maintain schisms in the proletariat.

In spite of the prohibition on workers' associations, various mutual-aid societies and resistance groups were forming. Immediately following the Paris and Lyons insurrections of April 1834 (some 1200 deaths occurred in Lyons in five days), the government forbade assemblies of twenty or more. The societies, in turn, went underground, for the movement by then had gathered too much momentum to be totally disrupted. Further clamping down came in 1835 with increased censorship of the press.

Journals representing a gamut of political persuasions proliferated at an accelerated rate in France during the 1830s. Between 1828 and 1846 male literacy rose by 52 percent as more and more workers found the means and energy to attend night classes.[7] They not only read such journals as *Le Globe*, *La Ruche Populaire*, *La Démocratie Pacifique*, and *La Phalange*, but some participated in bringing out these papers and wrote pamphlets, songs, and poems. By 1832, a new figure, the worker-poet, had appeared on the scene. When songs and poems were first introduced at workers' meetings, they met with rejection.[8] But by 1840 they must have become commonplace, for they had been discovered to be extremely effective in rousing the workers' spirit and sense of community (as Tristan was well aware; see her foreword to *The Workers' Union*).

By the end of the 1830s, many workers were in much direr straits than at the beginning of the decade. Not only had their demands for a minimum wage and a ten- or eleven-hour work day been ignored, but the deepening economic crisis and, to a lesser extent, the mechanization of production were creating greater numbers of unemployed and poverty-stricken individuals. It is

7. Michel Ragon, *Histoire de la littérature prolétaire en France* (Paris: Albin Michel, 1974), p. 82.
8. *Ibid.*, p. 84.

estimated that in December of 1839 some 150,000 people were out of work in Paris alone,[9] a labor situation of dangerous proportions when seen against an approximate total of 350,000 Parisian workers (*The Workers' Union*, chap. IV, n. 4). In 1840, numerous strikes took place with many arrests among tailors, shoemakers, masons, woodworkers, tanners, and haberdashers. Those who were not arrested were forced back to work by September of that year.[10]

At this time Flora Tristan brought out her stinging critique of Britain, which was published simultaneously in London and Paris. When re-edited in 1842, it was augmented with a dedication to the French workers exhorting them to recognize their plight and to prepare themselves for the struggle to come.

The Work

Upon publishing her vision of proletarian unification, *The Workers' Union (Union ouvrière),* Tristan proceeded to adopt one element from the otherwise rejected fraternal system. She borrowed its notion of the "French tour," a circuit traveled from town to town by the "companion" after his initiation into the brotherhood. Her missionary zeal in bringing the message of *The Workers' Union* personally and directly to the workers is recorded in a journal she had begun a year earlier and maintained until the end of September 1844.[11] The tour began officially on April 12, 1844, with her departure from Paris, although she had previously presented portions of her work to Parisian groups. A precious record, the journal functions as a companion piece to *The Workers'*

9. Edouard Dolléans citing Proudhon, in *Histoire du mouvement ouvrier 1830–1871* (Paris: Armand Colin, 1957), p. 181.

10. *Ibid.*, p. 184.

11. Flora Tristan, *Le Tour de France: Journal inédit 1843–1844* (Paris: Editions Tête de Feuilles, 1973). This was originally projected for publication in January 1845, but Tristan's death prevented that.

Union by detailing many of the circumstances involving the book's publication and dissemination. Additionally, it is a rich micro-social history providing descriptions of working conditions encountered in many towns, the townspeople's receptivity to Tristan's presence and ideas, meetings with various figures, and Tristan's personal reactions to what she saw and did. The journal also reveals a mystical approach to socialism. Fictionally foreshadowed in her novel *Méphis* and obliquely announced by an incident related in the *Promenades*,[12] this social evangelism had not been invoked in such intimate terms until the journal. In *The Workers' Union* the presence of Christ and his apostles prefigures Tristan's self-appointment as the modern female savior committed to rescuing the working poor from their intolerable circumstances.

Upon arriving in Auxerre, her first stop on the tour, she stated her conviction that she was expressly chosen to realize this mission: "I felt in me something like a divine grace enveloping, magnetizing, and transporting me into another life" (*Le Tour*, p. 38). Her health was not good from the start (she complained of digestive and gynecological problems), and it continued steadily to deteriorate; yet she could claim, "*Gods* [*sic*] needs me and keeps me from the sicknesses afflicting those who have nothing to do."[13] The pain resulting from her worsening physical condition and the frustration of not always communicating successfully with the workers became translated into a sense of martyrdom, a sublime submission to a transcendent cause. Not only did she compare herself with St. Theresa of Avila (*Le Tour*, p. 102), but she likened her role to that of Christ himself: "The Jewish people had died in abjection, and Jesus raised them up again. The Christian

12. While visiting the insane asylum of Bedlam, Tristan met a French inmate who proclaimed that she had been sent by God.

13. Tristan, *Le Tour*, p. 75. Her idiosyncratic rendering of God (Dieu) was *Gods (Dieux)*, reflecting her conception of a supreme being as a trinitarian generative principle containing the paternal, maternal, and the embryonic. Tristan uses this noun with singular verbs.

people are dead today in degradation and Flora Tristan, the first strong woman, will raise them up again" (*Le Tour*, p. 139).

Envisioned as history's first liberator or democratic leader of the masses, Christ served as a model for Tristan's task. She felt challenged to emulate his forthrightness and his ability to rally all the people around a common theme. For her, this ideological confidence and consolidation of the early Christian movement furnished the key to the unity necessary for both social change and maintenance of the faith. Thus the traditional notion of Christian love and devotion came to signify faith in humanity and belief in the people. In return, the kind of adoration emanating from the masses for their female savior was to resemble very closely the love a child would show its mother. Imbued with a kind of divine fervor, Tristan's caring was certainly a blend of maternal feelings, social activism, and evangelical zeal. In sum, as for Christ, the sacrificial giving of love defined the final martyrdom suffered. To a certain extent, Tristan was the expression of the more radical aspects of a certain political persuasion of the 1830s and 1840s in France: a vaguely religious, yet left-oriented movement called Christian humanitarianism, to which a number of writers and thinkers adhered, including George Sand.

The workers of Lyons, with their suffering and their history of organization and collective action, were the best prepared for Tristan's notions of unification and the construction of workers' palaces to harbor the young, the disabled, and the elderly. In Lyons she met with much working-class encouragement and as much bourgeois resistance. She also found a disciple, a young woman, Madame Eléonore Blanc, who was to become her first biographer. Blanc, a laundress, readily assumed the role of Tristan's spiritual daughter. But, in Tristan's critical eyes, Blanc's dedication was not consistently exemplary: an undesirable reaction on the part of her disciple could provoke very harsh judgment, giving Tristan a sense of increased isolation (*Le Tour*, pp.

142, 144)—the inevitable consequences of uncompromising principles.

This dual intensity—abundant love and extreme harshness—was also apparent in Tristan's attitude vis-à-vis the workers. On the one hand, and especially when particularly receptive to her speeches, the people were "full of good will, sensitivity, freshness, youth—precisely because they are not worn out" (*Le Tour*, p. 160, upon her departure from Lyons). But on the other hand, she sometimes lost patience and resorted to acerbic condemnation: "Nobody in the world would have the courage to live among such stupid beings. What's painful to see is that these wretched people think they are superior and are completely mistaken about their status" (*Le Tour*, p. 16, concerning some Parisian workers). The workers to whom she read sections of *The Workers' Union* resented her discussion of their drinking habits and tavern frequentation (chap. III, n. 10), but she refused to delete these critical passages. Even though she tended to refer to the workers in monolithic terms, the many encounters she related in the journal ultimately reveal occupational and geographical diversity. Nevertheless, for the sake of her activist argument she had to be able to proceed from certain generalities about an oppressed class, in order, first, to underscore the great need to improve the workers' general lot, and, second, to rally a massive effort to implement her project.

As she traveled from one place to the next making as many contacts as time and her physical condition would permit, Tristan was also being watched and followed by civil authorities. The surveillance escalated to more overt persecution, particularly in Lyons and Marseilles, where she spent the most time and had the greatest success in gathering the workers. An entry in her journal from June 1844 revealed her awareness of these activities: "I am furious. If I am not careful to hide all my papers, they are stolen. The police rented a room next to mine to spy on me; someone is always there listening close by to see if I forget and leave a paper or a note around; that makes three I have lost. What nastiness this spying is! Ah, the police will not forget my stay in Lyons." Upon her arrival in Toulon in late July, she was summoned to a police commissioner's office by order of the king's district attorney. Sick and tired of the surveillance and impingement upon her privacy, she recorded, "I said to his stupefied agent: tell the king's prosecutor that I don't have to report to his office; if he discovers I've committed a crime, he can subpoena me and then I'll appear." (*Le Tour*, pp. 191–92.)

In *The Workers' Union* Tristan claimed that she was not a revolutionary, no matter how her demeanor and activities might have appeared (in "To the Bourgeois"). She also claimed in her appeal to the bourgeois to be one of the "sighted" ones, those who saw the necessity of aiding the working class. How was this self-image to be reconciled with the subversive one projected by the authorities, the bourgeois themselves? How could she have been of the bourgeoisie, the dominant class, and yet have expected them to accept a challenge threatening their very order? These questions are best answered by focusing on Tristan's own brand of socialism, her particular vision with respect to social conditions.

If one understands Tristan's position as a bridge spanning several trends in social theory and praxis, rather than as a contradiction, then her true contribution comes to light. On the one hand, she was obviously a product of Social Utopianism; on the other, she opened the way for "scientific" socialism, the Marx-Engels formulation. Hers was a curious blend of materialistic perceptions and idealistic visions; and, appropriately, her writings and activism come historically at that moment of unfolding when the dreams and hopes of the 1830s merged with the growing revolutionary fervor that culminated in the events of 1848.

As mentioned earlier, among the Utopian Socialists, three demanded Tristan's close attention: Henri de Saint-Simon, Charles

Fourier, and Robert Owen.[14] For her, other Socialists tended to
be in small derivative schools founded by the formers' disciples
or were idiosyncratic, peripheral examples of progressive thinking.

With Saint-Simon (1760–1825) she shared a profound concern
for worker employment and education, with a belief in the necessity of the workers' *right* to work, his or her right to a decent
wage to be a matter of government determination.[15] Saint-Simon's
disdain for the idle rich and privilege was also hers,[16] but she did
not entertain his admiration for Napoleon Bonaparte.[17] His theory of progress inherited from eighteenth-century thinkers such
as Condorcet also underlies Tristan's general view of history,[18] as
she proposed a feminist-socialist equation to take up where Christianity left off in the linear progression of human events. Her
repeated use of the phrase "the most numerous and useful class"
to refer to the working masses was a deliberate echo and modifi-
cation of Saint-Simon's locution, "the most numerous and poorest class." Tristan's change of the second adjective reflected her
optimism along with her refusal to consider the working masses
as impoverished by definition (cf. chap. I, n. 2). Of those contemporaries for whom she professed admiration, many were Saint-
Simonians and appeared on her list of candidates as acceptable
"defenders" for the Workers' Union (chap. II).

Like Charles Fourier (1772–1837), with whom she had some
contact toward the end of his life, she feared the consequences of
industrial mechanization, the ultimate transformation of workers

14. The first sentence of Tristan's chapter on Robert Owen in the
Promenades stated categorically that she was not a Saint-Simonian,
Fourierist or an Owenian.

15. Henri de Saint-Simon, *Du Système industriel* (1820–21).

16. Henri de Saint-Simon, *L'Industrie*, vol. IV (1818), and *De La
Physiologie appliquée à l'amélioration des institutions sociales* (1825).

17. Henri de Saint-Simon, *Introduction aux travaux scientifiques du
dix-neuvième siècle* (1807–8).

18. *Ibid.*; Henri de Saint-Simon, *Extrait d'un ouvrage sur l'organisation sociale* (1804).

industrial mechanization, the ultimate transformation of workers
into dehumanized automatons or unemployed beggars. Her critical account in the *Promenades* of a visit to a British gas plant
suggests that she wholeheartedly agreed with his advocacy of
spacing out tedious, menial tasks and never requiring them for
more than a couple of hours at a time.[19] In her discussion of child
education, she specifically mentioned Fourier as a useful refer-
ence, his attractive phalansterian program serving as a model for
the union palaces Tristan wanted to institute.[20] She, too, would
impose an integral or combinative approach to education—equally
emphasizing the physical, the moral, and the intellectual—but
she would include as well an introduction to spiritual matters, a
respect for a providential deity, for which Fourier left no room.
Stressing vocational guidance and satisfaction in one's work, both
sought to rehabilitate manual labor, if not glorify it.[21] Of these
three major figures preceding Tristan, it was Fourier who specifically addressed the issue of woman's condition. His famous
statement (later picked up and re-phrased by Engels) to the effect
that the status of woman is the measure of society's evolution,
had also caught Tristan's attention.[22] It served as one of the epigraphs in her book on Britain.

The appeal of Robert Owen's socialism was elaborated in a
chapter devoted to him in the *Promenades*. His successful residen-
tial and laboring community of New Lanark, though much larger
in scale than the workers' union palace envisioned by Tristan,
stood as a testament to the feasibility of such experiments and
could only encourage her to adapt aspects of it to French proletarian needs. She highly approved of his program of nonsectarian
child education, the projects to provide labor for all adults, and

19. Charles Fourier, *Théorie de l'unité universelle* (1822).
20. *Ibid.*; Charles Fourier, *La Fausse Industrie morcelée* (1835–36).
21. Fourier, *Théorie de l'unité universelle*.
22. Charles Fourier, *Théorie des quatre mouvements et des destinées gé-
nérales* (1808).

labor organization as a political force.[23] Owen's infant schools for children between the ages of two and ten were based upon a progressive and empirical philosophy of education. No corporal punishment was allowed and children under the age of ten could not be employed. Visitors to New Lanark were impressed by their health and cheerfulness.

To maintain a certain level of enthusiasm among the two thousand workers who lived in New Lanark, a variety of tasks was required so that an industrial worker in the mill could also work in the communal garden. Because workers were not exploited in the capitalistic sense, the cost of production remained lower than elsewhere. Instead of a sixteen-hour day, in New Lanark workers labored ten and one-half hours. Even though their absolute wages were in fact lower than those of other workers, their standard of living was actually superior. The community could offer such benefits as staples at cost price and institutional meals to keep the cost of living in check. These were scarcely ideas or policies encouraged by French industrialists. Indeed, to illustrate the French aristocrat's abhorrence of the practical, artisanal education that Owenism advocated, i.e., the aristocrat's reluctance to value the work of the laborer, Tristan recalled a trial involving the controversial educational experience of a French youth sent to New Harmony, Indiana, where Owen's son, Robert Dale, had set up another community as the continuation of New Lanark (chap. II, n. 9).

Tristan's plan for the workers' palace, like Fourier's, was amazingly concrete in its series of precise details, yet somewhat vague in its general design. She vividly specified certain activities to be promoted in the palaces and even who might have preference for

23. Robert Owen: First, Second, and Third essays, and "An Address Delivered to the Inhabitants of New Lanark, January 1, 1816," in *A New View of Society; or, Essays on the Formation of the Human Character* (1818).

admission, but she oscillated on the actual dimensions of the institution. Initially, it was perceived simply to have a triple function: school for the young, refuge for the elderly, and infirmary for the sick and injured. But eventually it assumed larger proportions, a greater phalansterian look, with agricultural and industrial components encompassing more and more participants. Although she did not announce an expansionary approach, the institution seemed to grow and become more ambitious as the plan evolved.

If the workers' union palace derives much of its anticipated effect from some of the visions and experiments fostered by certain Utopian socialists, its projected implementation stemmed specifically from the social economy of France in the 1840s. Proletarian havens built by and for the workers would signal their unification, the organization of the working class. Insofar as Tristan recognized the necessity of a broad workers' association based upon class distinction, she moved in the direction of a more "scientific" kind of socialism. To the extent that her advocacy of proletarian action resided upon an economic and historical (materialist) analysis of society, she was one of the direct precursors of Marx and Engels. Pre-Marxian in her understanding of capitalism from the point of view of class consciousness and the problematic of general distribution of wealth, she formulated the reverse of the concept of surplus value with her notion of the *workers'* asset, their ownership of their laboring hands as distinct from the powers of capitalistic dominion over the employed (chap. II).

Philosophically, Tristan's materialism was not thoroughgoing, since her belief in divine providentiality constituted an idealistic cornerstone in her thinking. Her profound reverence for God's creation, the world and its inhabitants, was as much a product of Christian devotion as a purely social one. Furthermore, her attitude toward the Church was far from Marxist inasmuch as the religious institution was to be a source of aid and inspiration. This meant that Tristan, who refused to see the proletariat as invariably pitted against the rest of society, could scarcely be termed a communist revolutionary. While recognizing the inherent antagonisms of class society, she nonetheless advocated cooperation for peaceful reform, believing bourgeois and upper-class participation feasible and desirable in the workers' struggle. Her challenge did not attempt to subvert private enterprise or deny the manufacturer's right to compete for profits, and she did not call for the total dismantling of the economic order; she simply and soundly demanded a fair share for the laboring poor.

By reformulating the Utopians' legacy, by anticipating certain Marxian elements, and by transforming a visionary dream into a practical program for action, Tristan created a link, both in theory and in history, in the socialist chain of progressive action. *The Workers' Union* was the realization of the theoretical connection, which, in turn, summoned the first activist phase, reading the text. Tristan coordinated this process by personally supervising the book's publication and dissemination: not an easy task for a woman alone, hindered by a lack of resources and the enormous difficulty of making others take a woman seriously.

One of the longest chapters in *The Workers' Union* is devoted to the question of women, though addressed to men: "Why I Mention Women" (chap. III). By late twentieth-century standards, Tristan's feminism was less radical than her feminist-socialist equation. While she strongly urged education for girls (and placed her own daughter Aline as apprentice to a dressmaker to provide her with a skilled trade), this training was nevertheless to be adapted to a traditional view of woman's role. Child care was women's responsibility, but required preparation. Women were to receive some ethical education so as better to fill their role as guarantors of moral values, guardians of the domestic order. Even if employed outside the home, women were nonetheless domestically centered and essentially responsible for the nonfinancial well-being of their families. Since the fundamental familial structure went unchallenged in her analysis, the traditional division of labor remained virtually intact. Thus, woman as a political creature was not a prominent figure. Tristan assumed that the Workers' Union "defender" would be male. Furthermore, she did not address the question of female suffrage, an issue of increasing importance in the 1840s. One might argue that her endeavor to bestow upon women all the rights withheld since the French Revolution of 1789, though granted to men, subsumed the particular right to vote, but that right is not given any specific emphasis compared to education, employment (equal wages), and individual dignity or the right to live.

Countering the traditional (clerical) outlook that woman is "nothing," Tristan argued that woman is "everything in the life of the worker." Her reasoning sought, almost out of desperation in face of the special oppression suffered by women, to undermine the equation between female and victim, or marginal being. She seemed to sense that a women's movement would be more difficult to consolidate than the proletarian association, since class lines were not easily spanned. Of course, history has repeatedly borne out this intuition.

Tristan's refusal to assume a pseudonym exemplified in a more personal manner the close bond between theory and praxis she was able to establish through her writing and activism. She harshly criticized her contemporary who did take a male pen name, George Sand, née Aurore Dupin. The ease with which Madame Dudevant used male adjectives to describe herself suggests her awareness of the ingredients necessary for literary success in the man's world in which she lived. But for Tristan, the masculine pseudonym represented a refusal to identify *personally* with woman's subordinate position, indeed a rejection of feminist solidarity. This act of disguise thus diminished and neutralized the female experience.[24] According to Tristan, the fictionality of Sand's prose, coupled with the "veil" drawn by the pen name, constituted a

24. This criticism appears in the Preface to the *Pérégrinations d'une paria*; Sand's name is not stated but is easily inferred.

serious disjunction between writing and life, a rupture that could only weaken the impact of Sand's art upon her audience. Tristan chose to overlook the advantages of the fictional veil, which she saw as mere play bordering on falseness. This expression in favor of nonfiction certainly had something to do with her own failure as a novelist.

Since Sand and Tristan knew each other, another negative comparison between the two should be noted, specifically with respect to the question of notoriety. Sand's reputation has been both elevated and undermined because of the number of (well-known) lovers she had. Tristan, on the other hand, was equally notorious for *not* taking lovers after her escape from a disastrous marriage. With exotic and compelling good looks, Flora exasperated many willing suitors in her search for a pure and total commitment to bettering the plight of the "pariah." She even presided over a kind of "salon" in her apartment on the Rue du Bac, where the radical political ideas of the day were fervently discussed and where the notions elaborated in *The Workers' Union* were first tested. One might speculate that, in some remote fashion, Sand saw in Tristan a rival, a daring competitor whose uncompromising principles and unconventional lifestyle might have produced an even more flamboyant celebrity had Tristan lived beyond the age of forty-one. But Tristan's quest for fame was so thoroughly subjugated to her mystico-social commitment that the simple cult of personality cannot begin to describe her impulse. Nonetheless, she did incarnate in many ways the persona of the Romantic heroine: her exotic, aristocratic background, alluring charisma, striking appearance, and early death all highlighted a very dramatic existence. The energy and passion with which she undertook her travels, writing, and protests sublimely attest to the kind of "genius" revered by her contemporaries. Personal, yet persistently keyed into society and its betterment, Tristan's work is a salient example of feminist-socialist critique in its early phase.

Beverly Livingston

NOTE ON THE TRANSLATION

Some 140 years after Flora Tristan produced her works, they are beginning to find their way into English. Small segments of *The Workers' Union* have appeared in Italian,[1] and her books have been available in Spanish for a number of years, owing to Tristan's paternal heritage—her father's Peruvian background. In fact, in South America and specifically in Peru, Tristan is considered a native author, claimed as their very own early feminist-socialist. Though she never wrote in Spanish, she probably learned to converse during the months she spent in Arequipa on her uncle's estate.

As far as it is known, Tristan never benefited from any formal education. A self-taught social commentator, she submitted to publishers and printers manuscripts fraught with spelling errors and inelegant turns of phrase that had to be carefully corrected before going to press. In spite of these corrections, her style remains somewhat flawed. Her blocking of sentences and paragraphs is far from consistent, with a tendency, on the one hand, to accumulate everything into one sentence and, on the other, to bombard the reader with short paragraphs in staccato succession. In addition, her prose exhibits certain rhetorical accents common at the time, including exclamation, frequent repetition with little amplification, and simplistic generalities. Though quite characteristic of her generation, these devices seem to stem as well from the overflowing energy inspired by her need to get on with the practical work of implementing her ideas. As in any piece of

1. *La Lotta di Classe, antologia critica di scritti inediti, di teorici operai artegiani nel periodo 1830–1848 in Germania e in Francia* (Milan: Lavoro Liberato, 1975), 173–94.

propaganda, style is subordinated to the demands of the message, and the literary consequences of such an arrangement are usually all too salient.

To enhance the text's readability in English, I have intervened with some minor editing. The few simple stylistic changes were made only when the flow in English would have otherwise been seriously hampered. Along with the deletion of some exclamation marks, some other punctuation has been regularized to adhere to the standards of English prose. Clarity for the twentieth-century reader has been further maximized by omitting much of the original italicization. The tendency in political writing during the era of French Romanticism to underscore virtually everything actually results in a loss of emphasis. Therefore, I have taken the liberty of de-emphasizing in order to restore what I believe to be the fundamental accent in accordance with the text as a whole. All of Tristan's own footnotes have been retained and are placed at the ends of chapters. I have added some explanatory notes for references that might not be obvious to today's readers, and these are indicated with asterisks and placed at the bottom of text pages. All ellipses are as found in the original text.

Because *The Worker's Union* is essentially devoid of literary pretension and is overtly propagandistic, I have made no attempt to recreate a mid-nineteenth-century English style to render the original French. Moreover, the straightforwardness of Tristan's prose reveals little change when compared to French usage of today.

The translation is based upon the third and final edition to appear during Tristan's lifetime. All the paraphernalia accompanying the original have been kept intact and render the original precisely: the subscription lists for each edition, the various appeals directed to different segments of society, the songs and poems. The reader will also sense a stylistic leap upon leaving the three prefaces for the main body of the text. The prefaces provide an opportunity for Tristan as author, propagandist, and woman to express certain feelings about her project, its stumbling blocks and successes. In the central text, this personal note is relegated to an occasional footnote, for the dominant tone must lend credibility to her plan, i.e., it must be as logically "objective" as possible.

I have supplied a selective bibliography at the end.

Finally, but no less important, a special thanks is in order to the Andrew Mellon Foundation at the University of Pittsburgh for providing me with a postdoctoral fellowship, part of which was used to complete this project. Without this support for full-time research, the work of translation and annotation would have taken considerably longer.

The Workers' Union

---◆---

Today the worker creates everything,
does everything, produces everything,
and yet he has no rights, possesses
nothing, absolutely nothing.

(Adolphe Boyer)

Workers, unite—unity gives strength.

Preface to the Third Edition
(10,000 copies printed)

The rule of the masses is to show their opinion through *deeds*. They neither speak much nor write. They act. The deed—that is their argument.

It is useless then to make beautiful sentences about the Lyons workers' fervor for this little book *The Workers' Union*. Let us simply stick to relating the facts.

Several workers deeming it useful to have the little book spread among many in the working class had the idea of bringing out a third edition in Lyons, at the expense of the workers in Lyons, so to speak.

The small zealous group who came to propose this to me matched their words with their deeds by obtaining subscriptions at public meetings for 4,000 copies at 25 centimes each (1,000 francs).* Other groups formed which also got a certain number of subscriptions.

Through this process individualism has already begun to disappear. This time, instead of individuals' names appearing on the subscription list, we have *groups*, and only groups.

Workers! Yours is a great and beautiful thought—to group is to UNITE. That fact in itself proves that you have understood the little book's message—UNIONIZATION.

Brothers, you could not have shown me greater or more precious gratitude! Thus I am deeply touched. Encouraged by such

---

*The average worker earned roughly 20 centimes per hour; a seamstress made 150 francs annually. Rent per year for the typical worker was 200 francs; bread and milk per day cost 5 centimes.

a reward, I no longer fear weakening; no, I now know you have understood.

If the rivalries and hatred have already diminished; if enough agreement and brotherhood already exist among *all* men and women for groups to form, then what may we not hope for the future! Brothers, let us all repeat in unison: Unity gives strength. Only the union can SAVE us!

FLORA TRISTAN

Lyons, June 7, 1844

SUBSCRIPTION LIST

A group of working men and women completely devoted to the cause	1,000 frs.
A group of working women	50
A group of textile workers	100
A group of communist workers	100
A group of phalansterian workers	50
A group of sympathetic bourgeois	200
	1,500 frs.

Preface to the Second Edition

The Workers' Union having been published through the help and cooperation of a large number of persons, I must, as promised, give an exact account of all that has been morally and financially done since the publication of the first edition.

The principles and ideas put out in the little book have more deeply influenced the minds of intelligent workers than I had any reason to hope for. I shall simply relate the facts, leaving it up to the reader to judge the results. The reader will see how susceptible the workers, seemingly immersed in a deathly torpor, are to a sudden awakening when one comes and speaks to them about their real interests, their essential rights, and their dignity as free men, as *citizens* and *brothers*.

The little book went on sale on June 1, 1843. I sent copies to all the various guilds and to the Union Societarians.[1] I had 3,000 brochures distributed in the large workshops in Paris.[2] By July 10, I had already received 43 letters from workers, as many from Paris as from the provinces. Thirty-five workers belonging to various trades had come to me with the intention of offering their services for the cause. I accepted their good will and gave them the little book to sell to other workers. They all perfectly understood the importance I placed on having the book reach its proper destination, the workers.

I am pleased to see that the workers propagated the book with great zeal, and I must say that they had to show great dedication and much patience; for it is no mean task to convince the workers (I am speaking of the masses), to get them to understand certain basic ideas, and above all, to get them to read a serious book.

In the space of five months, workers sold between eight and

nine hundred copies to other workers. As of today, December 15, 1843, I have received 237 letters[3] from 87 workers, trade guilds and others, plus a large number of visits from workers, all coming to ask me how they might serve the cause.

Except for a few, all these letters are written in the same spirit and express the same feelings. In truth, it could not be otherwise, since only those who sympathize with my ideas wrote or came to see me. They all show their ardent desire to unite. "We are totally convinced," they say, "that unity gives strength; so we want with all our hearts to be able to unite. And we promise you that, in this regard, you will find us quite resolved to follow the good advice you give us in your little book. The only thing disturbing us is that it is very hard because each feels divided within himself."

Thus they all want to unite in order to be strong; today the workers all sense their weakness and suffer from their own isolation.

Now the whole truth must be told: the lofty, important questions of social economy treated in *The Workers' Union* have been understood by very few workers.

The French worker is a being apart. He has I know not what kind of love for the word *liberty*, which extends to exaltation and madness! The word *liberty*, imprinted upon his mind since 1789 by a mysterious, superhuman force (which up to now has been nothing but *a word*), dominates with the tyranny of an *idée fixe*. That is how the French worker is: he prefers to submit to unemployment, poverty, and hunger, rather than lose what he calls his liberty. So he pushed aside the idea of the right to work without even trying to examine it, because he fears that this right will entail a kind of regimentation. He wants no part of it and repulses it in horror. "Let me die of hunger," he cries, "but at least let me die *free!*"

For the six months that I have been speaking to workers, exhibiting a patience I did not think I was capable of, I tried every means to prove to them that the realization of the right to work, as I called it, would never bring about the regimentation they fear so much. But trying to reason with a man whose mind is possessed by an *idée fixe* is like trying to get the deaf to hear or the blind to see. The more you seek to persuade this man with good reasons, the faster his hobby horse gallops through his brain and hinders his understanding. So, thus far I have seen no results for my efforts.

Of all the means indicated in my book to improve the lot of the working class, one alone has readily captured the attention of all working men and women: the Workers' Union palace.

I find everyone in agreement on this point. And this is how I explain this agreement.

The French worker, this being apart, finds in his moral strength a courage that does not yet bear a name, but eventually it will be called *proletarian* courage. Armed with this nameless courage and impunity, he confronts the drudgery of fourteen- and sixteen-hour work days, all kinds of deprivations, suffering and grief of every sort. But he is made of iron and survives everything; and what's more, he is joyful, a practical joker who laughs at his own misery and sings to entertain himself. However, there are three misfortunes in the life of the French worker in the face of which his gaiety and philosophy fail: the welfare office, the hospice, and the beggars' cell.

Having to inscribe his name and address for some bread and a bundle of kindling, or having to send his wife or daughter to die in the hospice, or his elderly father to the beggars' cell . . . if the worker is forced to submit to these humiliations—and it happens!—totally abandoned by his courage, he despairingly sobs or bellows.

The French worker knows how to suffer, but he cannot beg: his pride prevents it. He is willing to bend beneath the weight of the enormous task imposed upon him, provided that he can hold his head high. Humiliation demoralizes him, removes his strength, kills him. For the French worker, there is a sword of Damocles both terrible and threatening: the welfare bureau, the hospice, and the beggars' cell.

By proving to the workers through a very simple fact (their number) that they possess in themselves immense wealth, that they, if they *want* to unite, can make millions with their pennies, and even more, that once in possession of this wealth, they could build huge farm-workshop-palaces for themselves, both grandiose and pleasing, I delivered them from the humiliation of the alms and gave them a glimpse of paradise!

To explain the unanimity on the palaces: In all the workers' letters, the *palace* is the main issue. Owning a lovely dwelling, their very own, being able to raise their children, taking in workers disabled on the job, and finding a respectable retreat for their retirement are happy prospects that move them greatly. They all speak to me about the palace with emotion and enthusiasm, expressing hope and joy. Thus I can affirm here that *all* the workers want and are ready to cooperate, each according to his means, in the realization of the workers' union palace. This is the little book's effect on the workers' minds.

Now, let us consider the bourgeois. I must say, in praise of them and to the general surprise of the workers, that I found aid, sympathy, and approval among the bourgeois. Both men and women belonging to the upper bourgeoisie, nobility, and even clergy have written very nice letters showing their sincere interest in the working class. These people have come and shown me they would like to serve the workers' cause. Several have sent me sums of money for the cause. Don't all these demonstrations obviously prove that the enlightened segment of the bourgeoisie would be disposed to helping the workers when the latter want to try to unite?

I am going to cite some passages from letters I received upon the publication of my book. By showing the approval given to my idea by men of the highest merit, I hope to attract the attention of those who have not been persuaded by the logic of my reasoning.

Madame,

I am touched, more than I can tell you, by the generous sentiments expressed in your letter and the interesting book you kindly sent me. Your profound empathy for the social misery we see everywhere has always moved me; and if I have only imperfectly succeeded in what I have attempted, nothing is sweeter to me than to see the sincerity of my efforts recognized by someone who judges everything with both her heart and mind.

Indeed, I will in no way dissuade you from pursuing the great and noble enterprise you have begun! There are too many people today who assume every generous feeling to be *illusion* and every social or political reform to be *utopia*. Moreover, I am quite convinced that there is a well of truth in your project, as well as the principle behind a new and very healthy institution for the working classes. The organizational difficulties to be conquered are very great. Besides the obstacles inherent in all creations. There are impediments coming from the authorities, legal problems, difficulty in obtaining resources, using and distributing them, etc. It is nonetheless true that the creation of a large asylum, called a *Palace* or otherwise, for the laboring sick is a beautiful concept; and that the best means for reaching this goal is for all the working classes to contribute. This notion can be modified, restricted, expanded, or applied in various ways which would have to be discussed. But, I repeat, to my way of thinking, this is the seed for the foundation of a great institution. Therefore, should you be kind enough to give some importance to my opinion, permit me to offer you my ardent and sincere approbation. . . .

Allow me to express my thoughts. I am convinced that each day we shall see the number of voices grow in defense of the laboring classes, deserted for so long. It is a question of morality and justice that, once exposed, cannot be ignored. It is a cause won simply by being discussed. But rest assured, Madame, the best lawyers for this noble cause will be those who will defend it without payment. Some of them might be very loathe to receive any remuneration for their efforts, however legitimate. And our society is such that the voice of the defenders would be less powerful if it were believed to be self-interested. O'Connell's example should not fool us.* A *national pension* was given to him not so much to help him serve Ireland, but as a reward for having served his country (or rather it had this dual purpose). When the Irish people honored him with a national salary, O'Connell had already been rendering services larger than any man had ever given his country—for more than ten years. Certainly nothing can be done to benefit the best of causes without a lot of money; but it would be the association alone, if and when it is formed, which ought to be the recipient in order that it may act in the common interest. Besides, this is a matter to be deliberated at length. As for me, Madame, I am totally involved in other work and can only be associated from afar with these intentions whose excellence I recognize. I am, moreover, quite convinced that before they are implemented, the good ideas contained in your book need to be exposed to public debate. And I know no better apostle for these ideas than the one who has conceived of them.

Gustave de Beaumont
(Deputy from La Sarthe)

. . . Your idea has much grandeur and power, but it is a *utopia* and I shall prove it to you. For *internal* and *external* reasons it is not possible for it to be realized given the current state of affairs in France. But I do believe that the production of the idea is good, provided that it be wrapped in a cloak of great social charity and not revolt. Let us understand each other: be severe, strongly defend the rights dishonored; but no hatred, no talk of war. The bourgeois are also people, and the masses' emancipation must be done more intelligently, more scientifically, and more Christianly than that of the bourgeoisie.

. . . I do not encourage you to pursue the implementation of

* O'Connell's example is further discussed in Chapter II.

your idea right now. Deliver it up; come back to it from time to time. And each time, if it smiles to enlightened workers, as I think it will, you will take that opportunity to inoculate them with good ideas and lofty feelings.

. . . I think, in so doing, you will have assumed an excellent position, and you will be able to use it to do much good. Whatever the outcome of your project, your efforts will have some influence upon the workers. At least, that is my way of seeing it.

Victor Considérant
Editor-in-Chief,
La Démocratie Pacifique

Dear Lady, reading your little book has given me great pleasure. Your work is admirable for its charitable and *logical* thinking, and I understand all the joy you must feel in having done it.

. . . Your book has immense *practical* worth. It is not simply an expression of pure theory and doctrine taught a hundred times in vain; it is an *act*, and one of the highest importance. We have discussed enough, now we must *act*, under pain of stagnating or even regressing. Pure speculation has never achieved striking progress or a revolution in this world. Only *action* has that power. A few poor preachers full of faith have done more for the good of humanity than all the philosophers together. As I have already told you, for me, the whole problem of today is the question of finding means of implementation, action. I am happy to see you take this route and especially advise *peaceful* means. The men you call *reasonable*, distinguishing them from the "enthusiastic" and the "believers," might very well envy the practical, profound reasoning and intelligence of your views and proposal. The plan is simple, like all great things: it contains the seed for a thousand reforms whose *theoretical* necessity is denied by no one. It is especially excellent in that it can be achieved without violent upheaval or by alarming the *dominant interests*. On the other hand, with a little reflection, it can be easily seen that all these interests ought to form a coalition for its implementation. For the gradual and peaceful liberation of labor must necessarily turn in their favor, according to the simplest laws of economics.

You will have the glory of being the first to formulate a rich idea, whence the most meaningful consequences. No matter what its reception, your idea will always be usefully productive.

A. A. . . . r

Attorney at the Royal Court of. . . .

I shall not discuss with you the high questions of political economy in your book; I have not studied them enough. And if you want me to tell you my whole thought, I believe them to be *premature*. But I was struck by one point, because I think it is realizable; I want to speak of the *palaces*. In my opinion, this is the most remarkable aspect of your work. The hospice no longer suits our times; that word clashes with the word *citizen*, and the lowest beggar is, despite his poverty, *a citizen*. The single word *palace*, as opposed to hospice, old people's home, or any other denotation, seems innovative to me. What debases the people is that they believe they are destined to be debased. The first thing to do then would be to raise them in their own eyes. The people think that the wealthy scorn them; they are wrong: I am wealthy and I live among the wealthy, and I can affirm that we have more esteem and respect for them than they show for themselves. . . . I think the high society ladies, and particularly those of the aristocracy, would do at least as much (and maybe more) to hasten the construction of those palaces as they recently did for the disaster victims in the Guadeloupe.* One or two well-placed, active women would be enough to get it started. Then it would be in style, and in a few weeks the funds needed for the first palace could be collected. . . .

You see, Madame, it is up to you as the creator of the idea to get us to serve it. As for me, you will always find me ready to work for the good of my brothers. As soon as you have organized a society, committee, or some other mode of action, I shall be

* In 1836 and 1837 the volcano La Soufrière erupted, causing widespread devastation.

pressed to put my good will, activity, and some financial resources at your disposal, which I shall be happy to be able to
offer for such kind work.

                                                    Amélie de D. . . .

Madame,

Permit me to tell you how struck I was by the great, practical,
and fertile ideas which distinguish your beautiful, eloquent work
on the *Workers' Union.*

The admirable example of Ireland shows what power the masses
can attain by joining together, without going beyond legal limits.
It seems to me that the more society's working classes tend to
band together, to unite their efforts, interests, modes of action,
the more weight and authority their legitimate demands will have.
It is in that respect, Madame, that your proposal to build Workers' Union *Palaces* appears all the more excellent because it is
achievable, immediately achievable. . . .

Thus, with minimal donations, the workers could begin as of
today to build the foundation of one of these edifices you perfectly described, Madame: vast establishments where children
would receive vocational training and the elderly a respectable
retirement home.

This initiative taken by the working class would have, I think,
a huge impact, and I can assure you, Madame, that several of my
friends and I, as subscribers to the building of the first Workers'
Union palace, would be proud and pleased to help this praiseworthy enterprise with our deep concern, ardent aid, and what
financial means might be available.

Have courage and hope, Madame; the sacred cause you have
so wholeheartedly and selflessly dedicated yourself to is in preparation. The workers' cry of grief and misery has reached as far
as the upper echelons of society. It would be a blasphemy on
humanity to think that so many tears will not be finally wiped,
so much resignation made up for, so much hard labor glorified
. . . By *uniting*, the working classes can hasten that happy day
. . . . HELP YOURSELF . . . AND HEAVEN WILL HELP YOU . . .

                                                    Eugène Sue

Here is a passage from a letter from Monsieur Blanqui: he is responding to a worker who, on behalf of his comrades, had expressed their desire to contribute to a palace or a retirement home for the workers.

. . . . Your project seems excellent to me; it is simple and practicable from every point of view, a matter of order and will. If you ever manage to build a workers' retirement home through voluntary subscriptions, which I believe in and hope for, you will have solved an immense problem. *You can do it.* It will be the most beautiful Hôtel des Invalides of our time. One must want it and persevere. Remember that nine-tenths of the taxes paid annually are under ten francs! If millions are made from pennies, so you can establish something serious with small subscriptions not exceeding the worker's ability to pay.
. . . Thus, sir, I cannot be overly approving of the great experiment you are attempting. Rest assured that, when the time comes and your subscription is well established, the country will come to your aid.

By the tone of these letters, it can be seen that, if the workers *wanted to unite*, they could be certain of finding active and powerful cooperation among the bourgeoisie.

Encouraged by the concerns of noble and generous souls, I am going to redouble my efforts to fulfill in a worthy fashion the task I have undertaken. But it must be understood that if I am left alone to carry such a heavy burden, no matter how great my faith and good will, I shall fall exhausted from it.

I am addressing women in particular, because given the current state of affairs, they can serve the cause more effectively than men. But it is to intelligent women who are God-loving and humanitarian that I appeal.

So I come to appeal to people motivated by a saintly dedication. In the name of the good work, I ask them to be willing to help me morally and materially.[4]

One must finally stop confusing charity with alms.[5] For more than two thousand years, the Jews and Christians have been giving alms—and there are still beggars among them.

So, if the Catholic priests in France can find thousands of rich, noble women to be their ladies of alms, then why not hope to find a few hundred intelligent and dedicated ladies in this same country who would consider it a duty, an honor, to become women of charity?

Let us examine how their mission would be different. The ladies of alms go to the homes of the rich to request alms for the poor; then they go to the poor to distribute the aid. They also go to prisons to speak to prostitutes, thieves, and criminals; they get work for them, place them when they get out, etc. Of course, it is honorable to take on such a mission; but what are the results? Nil! Because the aid cannot eradicate poverty; prostitution, theft, and crime are its inevitable consequences.

The women of charity, on the other hand, would go to the rich to show them that it is their duty and in their interest to work for the eradication of poverty to get rid of prostitutes and criminals. They would prove to them that it is possible, if they would regularly pledge for ten years what they give each year in various alms. By their numbers, they would prove to them that in totaling the alms given in France as individual, separate aid, one could create manufacturing and agricultural jobs on a large scale in less than three years, so as to ensure a decent livelihood for *every* man and woman. Then, they would go to the workshops, to instruct the workers in town and country about their rights, duties, and other interests. The ones who are talented enough could give classes. The ones who are wealthy enough could support the fervent, active, and intelligent unionists whose task it would be to go everywhere possible to spread the word.

In my opinion, this is a sacred, sublime mission worthy of the truly charitable and religious woman.

In the name of God's love in humanity I appeal to and implore intelligent women to establish *the order of women of charity*.[6]

Now let us take a look at financial matters.

Fifteen hundred copies of the book have been sold, most for 25 or 30 centimes (because of the discounts one has to give).

From other sources.	500 fr.
The others have been placed *in good hands.*	
Remaining from the first subscription.	616 fr.
Expenses for mailing, posters, brochures (12,000), etc.	
	496 fr.
Remainder	120 fr.
	620
New subscriptions,	1,104 .50
Total	1,724 .50

I have just had 10,000 copies of the second edition printed which cost 2,200 francs all told.

In the third edition, I shall account for these 10,000 copies.

Paris, January 20, 1844

NEW LIST OF SUBSCRIBERS

	Francs
1. Mlle. Aline Tristan	20
2. Marie-Madeleine, maid	1
3. Jules Laure, painter	20
4. Five curriers	10
5. Pierre Vandervoort, businessman	20
6. Three actresses	18
7. Mme. A. Arnaud, author	5
8. Hawre, painter	10
9. Constant Berrier, playwright	5
10. Cantagrel, journalist	10
11. An artist	5
12. L., entrepreneur	10
13. Eugène C.	5
14. Victor Stouvenel	5
15. V.B.	10
16. Mlle. Marie de S.	10
17. The Marquis de L.	20
18. Julien, from Paris	5
19. Dr. R.	10
20. F.	5
21. Ganneau	1
22. O.-N., Deputy	10
23. Dr. Recurt	5
24. An Italian refugee	5
25. Prudhomme, bookseller	5
26. Dépaulle, painter	5
27. Delloye, publisher	5
28. By M. Michel's manual labor	12
29. Augustin, employee	5
30. Anonymous	5
31. Two laundrywomen	4

		Francs
32.	A businessman	5
33.	Moyses, businessman	2
34.	Several workers together	30
35.	Mme. Pauline Roland	5
36.	Surbled	5
37.	An officer	2
38.	Benoit, broker	3
39.	Two unionists	10
40.	Desroches, mining engineer	10
41.	Anonymous	40
42.	Saive, hatmaker	.50
43.	de S., peer of France	10
44.	Auguste Audemar, lawyer	20
45.	Duverger, printer	5
46.	Victor Brisson	5
47.	F.	5
48.	Bourrin, servant	5
49.	Princess Christine Belgiojoso	20
50.	R. Celse Pareto, architect	10
51.	Joseph Cornero, lawyer	10
52.	Dr. B.	10
53.	Moriceau, lawyer	5
54.	Colonel Bory de Saint-Vincent	15
55.	César Daly, architect	10
56.	C. Pecqueur	2
57.	L., landlord	300
58.	Philippe Benoist, painter	5
59.	A. Bayot, painter	5
60.	T.H., landlord	7
61.	Edme, mechanic	2
62.	Mme. Sophie C. D.	5
63.	Dubois, typesetter	2
64.	Schiller, printer	1
65.	Eugène Sue	20
66.	Gérard Séguin, painter	10
67.	Mlle. Ernest Gérard, voice teacher	5

	Francs
68. An officer	5
69. L.	5
70. J.C.	5
71. By M. Legallois's manual labor	25
72. Charles F., student	5
73. An officer	3
74. Victor Hennequin, lawyer	5
75. A priest	3
76. Anonymous	5
77. Adolphe Legrand	10
78. Charles Goubault	5
79. Frodet, professor	3
80. A. Latour, professor	2
81. Léon	5
82. J::M::J, workers	20
83. Raynier, silkworker	2
85. Marc Fouger, locksmith	2
86. L. V. Isore, Jr., mason	2
87. Julien Grosmen, tawer	2
88. A Polish lady	5
89. Anonymous	5
90. De la Suhardière	5
91. Mme. Hortense de Méritens, author	5
92. Worms, printer	10
93. Escalère, Sr., businessman	10
94. Gustave Jourdain, student	3
95 F., sculptor	3
96. Deloin	1
97. De T., Deputy	20
98. Jules Lovy	10
99. A. Thys	10
100. Edouard de Pompéry	5
101. Blanqui, Director, School of Commerce	15
102. Mlle. Maxime, actress	10

1,104.50

NOTES

1. Here is the letter I sent them:
Dear Sirs:
I am mailing you a copy of the little book, *The Workers' Union*,
and I beg you to be kind enough to read, discuss, and study as
attentively as possible the questions I have treated.

I am outside any coterie or cult of personality. Thus it is solely
from the point of view of the *common good* that I have treated the
issue of the *union among all workers*. As far as I am concerned,
there are neither *"gavots"* nor *"dévoirants"* [members of enemy
guilds who battled violently against each other], only equal men,
citizens with the same rights and the same interests, unfortunate
brothers needing to love each other and unite to claim peacefully
their rights and defend their interests.

Gentlemen, I entreat you to read my little book impartially.
Do not let yourselves be blinded by any fatal, absurd prejudice.
May my being a woman not be reason to push aside my work.
Realize that love, intelligence, and strength have no sex. In reading *The Workers' Union*, do not be concerned only with studying
the value of its ideas. If you judge them to be good, rational, and
realizable, cast me aside and make them your own. What I aspire
to is not the vain glory of having written a book. No, praise the
Lord! I am above that pettiness. What I want and what I am
working for is to serve effectively the largest and most useful
class. That is all I want and nothing more.

As you will see in my preface, the sale of this little book is not
a commercial venture. Any money that comes from it will be
used to serve the cause. That is why, Gentlemen, I come openly
and fraternally to ask you to help me place the book among the
workers. I am requesting your support for the cause, not for
myself. If, in a year from now, we manage to get every worker a
copy of *The Workers' Union*, in three years, the universal union of
men and women workers will be possible, and then, my brothers,
we will be saved.

Cordial greetings from your *sister in humanity*.

Flora Tristan

P.S. See how many copies you think you can place among the workers and let me know. I shall send them via a peddlar or a coachman to avoid postal costs, which are high. When you have sold them all, you can have the money forwarded.

2. The brochure was a résumé of what is on page 128.

3. I did not receive a single letter from a working *woman*. However, two young laundresses came to see me on their own and each offered to bring me two francs every three months to be used in the service of the cause. And a third working-class woman was brought to me. No other signs from working women. Thus that makes three women to eighty-seven men.

4. I invite those interested in my work kindly to get in touch with me at 89, rue du Bac, in Paris.

5. Charity—love for God; the most perfect of the three theological virtues. Love, fervor, kindliness for one's fellow man. (Dict.) Alms—refers especially to money; to give alms, to live on charity, to be reduced to beggary, to be on charity. (Dict.)

6. From *La Démocratie Pacifique* of November 26, 1843:

"Here is an example that deserves to be pointed out to the clergy of France and Europe, living proof of the intellectual progress being made in the very midst of the Catholic hierarchy. Honor to the Cardinal and Archbishop of Malines, who thinks that Christian charity should not be limited to giving alms, but that it must above all be concerned with providing jobs.

" 'Reverend Fathers:

" 'In his letter of last September 16th, the Minister of Justice informed me that in order to relieve the working classes' malaise, the government has called the provincial authorities' attention to the advantages that would be effected for the indigent by organizing trade and apprentice workshops or factory schools, as well as by establishing aid committees to obtain materials and jobs for needy workers. The Minister adds that it would be desirable, in the purely agricultural communities, for the welfare bureaus to agree with the municipal authorities to replace free aid with wages by hiring the poor workers to clear uncultivated land or to repair local roads, in order to maintain the habit of work and to provide them with some means of existence. . . .

" 'You know, Reverend Fathers, that, although the salvation of souls is the aim of our sacred ministry, we must want to contribute as well to the physical well-being of our fellow man and alleviate his worldly needs, all the more because it is a very effective way to get him to love religion.'

"This letter is remarkable both for its reasonableness and its evangelical spirit. It contains two eminently religious principles that are in agreement with scientific fact.

"The first is that the giving of alms must be changed. Charity has to prevent poverty rather than alleviate it. In the social process, alms can only be considered as accessory; the object is for the poor classes to use their hands productively. Labor organization is essential and fundamental; welfare organization can only be temporary and subsidiary.

"The second principle is that the Christian religion, while chiefly concerned with saving souls, must nonetheless contribute to the material well-being of the people."

Preface to the First Edition

Because this little book is outside the usual flow of things and because of a peculiar fact, I must provide an explanation.

Judged by his established reputation, shouldn't Monsieur Pagnerre,* the only popular publisher remaining, bring out *The Workers' Union?*

Indeed, everyone said, "Monsieur Pagnerre is the only publisher who can take on your work." I thought so, too. So without hesitating, I went to see him; I sent him part of my manuscript (the first three chapters) telling him that the book belonged with him in its spirit, goal, and topic. Here is his reply.

Paris, March 31, 1843

Dear Madame,

I am returning the proofs you kindly sent me; I regret that the work to which I have to devote all my time and care does not allow me to aid in the publication of your book. The goal you propose is praiseworthy and generous, and, even though I do not share all your opinions on the means of improving the workers' situation, I nonetheless sincerely wish you well in order that all the projects tending toward that result will be examined, seriously discussed and put in practice, if need be.

Sincerely yours,
Pagnerre

If Monsieur Pagnerre, the publisher for the lions of democracy and popular publisher par excellence, refused to bring out *The*

---

* Laurent-Antoine Pagnerre (1805–54) participated in the 1830 Revolution, served as General Secretary of the Provisional Government of 1848, and later as Deputy to the Constituant.

Workers' Union, no other hope remained of finding another publisher who would be willing to take it on. However, since I still needed one, I went to three or four more. They all sent me back to Monsieur Pagnerre, saying, "He is the only one who can publish this type of work, because it is in his field."

I have several reasons for recalling this:

1. I wished to respond to the query, "Why didn't you have your book published by Pagnerre?" (Already everyone is asking me.) "With him you would have been assured of good sales; his contacts are very numerous; your book would have been placed in good hands. You have made a mistake, and *The Workers' Union* will lose out for it." Thus, Pagnerre's letter replies to those who might be tempted to reproach me for this.

2. Furthermore, the refusal contains an important lesson. It proves how false established reputations often are. In a hundred years, writers on the reign of Louis-Philippe will present Monsieur Pagnerre as the popular publisher of the era. Poor people! Nowadays there is not even one publisher who will agree to publish a little book whose goal is to defend the interest of the working class.

3. Also another lesson comes out of this refusal, which is that, more than ever, intelligence is being subordinated to purely material ways.

My position was becoming very difficult. I needed between 1,000 and 2,000 francs to publish the work, and I did not have it. Paying one's own publishing costs quickly exhausts one's limited resources. For several days I endured a torture known only by those who live in the realm of the mind. I was aware of the goodness and usefulness of the ideas I had just put to paper, and it was poignantly painful to think that those ideas were going to stay there, like a dead letter, for lack of a 1,000-franc note. But when God grants faith to an individual, He gives it fully and wholly.

After three or four nights of painful insomnia, I was very

surprised one morning to feel quite calm and confident, and stronger than ever.

From my window I can see the towers of Saint-Sulpice. Given my state of mind, the sight of that beautiful church had a special effect on me. It immediately reminded me of all the great, generous, and sometimes sublime actions that faith had inspired in the Christians. "Well!" I thought, "*my religion*, which is just as sublime, is to love my brothers in humanity; *my faith* is to love and serve God in humanity. With consequences so beautiful and pure, wouldn't it give me as much strength and power as the Catholics have, loving God and serving the poor in view of heavenly compensation?" Well, a priest, a man alone but confident in his faith, took it upon himself to build one of the most beautiful churches in Paris, Saint-Sulpice. And to reach his goal, he was undaunted by neither fatigue nor humiliation; he went from door to door collecting for his church. And with small alms this great, magnificent church was raised majestically into the air.[1] And couldn't I, following the priest's example, go from door to door asking for subscriptions to publish a little book for the instruction of the largest class of people? Were I to hesitate or draw back from this noble task, I would be tacitly recognizing the nullity of the religion I profess. This would be a denial of the God I serve. In a word, it would be a confession that may faith is *not* as powerful as that of the Catholics.

How happy are they who have faith!

At that very moment I felt inflamed by a love so great, a force so powerful, that neither fatigue nor humiliation would ever frighten me again. I decided to go from door to door myself, until I had the necessary 1,200 francs. This plan came to mind so suddenly that it seemed as if a foreign will not my own had ordered me to act: Take a big sheet of paper and write at the top: *Appeal to all intelligent and dedicated people*—we are asking their help to have *The Workers' Union* published. Then: write my name first, get my daughter to sign, my maid, my water carrier; run right

away to my friends to explain my resolution. All that took only
twenty-four hours.

I must make it known that my task was very difficult in a way
different from the priest's. For him it was a question of the Catholic union; and he was certain to find aid, sympathy, welcome,
confidence, approval, and praise almost everywhere; whereas I
was acting independently and with the quasi-certainty that I would
be generally poorly received.

Since I am trying to show the lesson resulting from all this, let
me enter into greater detail. I was soliciting in order to publish a
book intended to instruct the working class. After asking my
friends, I naturally then went to all those who seemed true friends
and ardent defenders of the people. Oh, how many cruel disappointments awaited me!

I shall name no names here, but it will be seen by the absence
of certain ones on my subscription list that, except for a few
"friends of the people," it was exactly as it had been with Monsieur Pagnerre, the only difference being that he was extremely
polite in refusing me. Whereas among the "friends of the people,"
several barely received me politely (three or four even refused to
see me), and refused to participate on no uncertain terms.

What is the explanation for this?

May each interpret in his or her own way; for the moment, I
shall limit myself to observing the facts.

This is not the place to relate how these cold, dry, and completely antifraternal receptions caused me sharp pain; how often
tears of indignation burned my cheeks upon leaving the homes of
those "friends of the people," who always have the grandiose
word *fraternity* at the tip of their pens.*

---

* Elsewhere, in a list of people who refused to contribute, Tristan
mentions Eugène Delacroix, Lamennais, Chateaubriand, Lafitte, Baron
de Rothschild, and the actresses Mars and Rachel; cited by Jules-L.
Puech in *La Vie et l'oeuvre de Flora Tristan 1803–1844* (Paris: Marcel
Rivière, 1925), p. 445.

Poor people! Your so-called friends are using you . . . and at bottom, none of them really intends to be of use to you.

Nor shall I speak of the courage I needed to persevere in accomplishing my task. In times like these of egotism and Robert-Macairism,* to go to people who do not know you and request money for a book to teach the people their rights was, indeed, the execution of a veritable *tour de force.*

Jesus was right when he said, "Have faith and you will move mountains." I have just experienced for myself that he spoke the exact truth. For almost the whole month that my apostolic life lasted (actively), I did not feel discouraged for a minute. And yet, how many disappointments didn't I suffer, without counting the crude rebuffs of certain *nouveaux riches* who thought I was simply a poor woman of letters asking for charity. It would be very curious to relate all the strange and comical scenes that happened to me. Later, I shall reveal how much the moral and physical fatigue of this act of great charity cost me. I do not exaggerate in saying that I ran more than *two hundred* errands all over Paris (and on foot). I confess that I am physically exhausted; I am even ill. But I hasten to add that amidst all these troubles, I did have many joys. I found people with great and generous souls, whom I had never counted upon, wishing ardently to be able to do good. And understanding all the beauty of my mission, they showed me kindness and respect. The few moments of conversation with these people completely made up for all the disappointments the others caused me.

On the one hand, what I have said about the supposed friends of the people might astonish and sadden some people naïve enough to judge a man's heart by the writer's beautiful sentences. On the other hand, the workers especially might be surprised to learn that the bourgeois with aristocratic manners very sympathetically

---

* Robert Macaire, a stock character and subject of many plays in the French popular theater of the 1830s and 1840s, epitomized the rogue or scoundrel.

received my idea and contributed generously. As for the artists, almost all gave me a warm welcome, and only three refused to offer anything.

Now, I must say, in order to avoid the wrong impression, that none of the persons who signed my list and pledged a gift knew the contents of my manuscript.[22] Consequently, none can be held responsible for the ideas in it.

The faith motivating me as I spoke to them gave them faith in me. They saw me so deeply convinced of the goodness of my work that they in turn became convinced that I could not do any harm. And often, without requesting any explanation, they gave me help.

If the ideas in my book are too advanced or are expressed in such a way as to wound certain vulnerable minds, I beseech those who have honored me with their kind cooperation to trust that I never intended to undermine their confidence. I firmly believe that I am sending the public a good and useful book. If I am wrong or misled, I attest that my intentions were pure and loyal and that I am acting in good faith.

Now, let us discuss financial matters.

By means of gifts and subscriptions, I was able to have *The Workers' Union* typeset, printed, and plated. The book is but a small property. However, if the workers understand its impact, a large number of copies will be sold. Then this property's value will increase more or less. I herewith promise never to use the income from this property for my personal benefit. My intention is to produce other small books whose goal will be the same: to instruct the working classes.

As for the first edition (4,000 copies), it will bring in practically nothing, and this is why. First of all, it will be necessary to give away a great many copies to donors. Then, I shall send some to all the trade guilds and the Union Society, etc. Some will also have to be sent to people in all walks of life. As I want to make the *idea* known, I think about 3,000 copies will be distributed this way. Moreover, with the second edition, I shall account precisely for the 4,000 copies of the first printing, and each donor will receive a new copy.

I am going to provide the subscription list. Several people have wished to remain anonymous, and I have respected their wish. Others wanted only their initials. As much as possible, I have indicated the status or profession of everyone in order to show that I contacted all social classes. As for the Deputies in the legislature, I felt that I should not publish any of their names, in order to leave them totally free to attack or support the book's ideas.

SUBSCRIBERS

		Francs
1.	Mme. Flora Tristan	100
2.	Mlle. Aline Tristan, dressmaker	5
3.	Jules Laure, painter	20
4.	Marie-Madeleine, maid	1.50
5.	Adolphy, landscape architect	10
6.	Ed. R., investor	10
7.	Dr. E., from several friends	100
8.	Colonel Bory de Saint-Vincent	10
9.	De la Suhardière	5
10.	G. de B., Deputy	30
11.	S., Deputy	20
12.	A soldier	1.50
13.	Noël Taphanel, water carrier	.50
14.	P. J. de Béranger	10
15.	Victor Considérant	10
16.	Desroches, engineer	10
17.	L., Deputy	25
18.	Widow Augendre, laundress	1
19.	Marie Mouret, maid	.50
20.	Anonymous	.50
21.	A priest	2
22.	Alphonse Masson, painter	10
23.	H. Raimond, landlord	5
24.	S., Peer of France	15
25.	Anonymous	5
26.	Ch., businessman	200
27.	L., Deputy	5
28.	Marteau, concierge	.50
29.	Mme. Dumoutier	5
30.	Jules Delécluse, businessman	3
31.	Décheveaux-Dumesnil, clockmaker	.50
32.	B. Levillain, attorney	1
33.	G. C.	10
34.	Guérin, landlord	40

	Francs
35. Renaud, landlord	10
36. Dr. Voisin	20
37. Edouard de Pompéry	5
38. Eugène Sue	100
39. Mme. J. Lormeau	1.50
40. George Sand	40
41. V. Schoelcher	40
42. P.F.	10
43. Mlle. Joséphine Fournier	.50
44. Anonymous	100
45. Murs. de Marliani	10
46. C., Deputy	20
47. M. Raba, landlord, Honor of Legion	20
48. de B., Deputy	10
49. Jules Lefèvre, author	5
50. Rossi	10
51. Gen. Jorry	.50
52. Eustache J.	10
53. Charles Poncy, mason from Toulon	3
54. Phiquepal d'Arusmont	25
55. Mme. Hortense Allart	5
56. Arsenne, painter	10
57. Etex, sculptor	5
58. Mme. Pauline Roland	5
59. Blanqui, Director, School of Commerce	15
60. Bocage, actor	20
61. Frédérik-Lemaître, actor	10
62. Agricol Perdiguier, cabinetmaker	3
63. Vezé, businessman	.50
64. De L., Deputy	10
65. Mme. Sophie D., stockholder	5
66. Jacques Legrand, hatmaker	1.50
67. H.D., Deputy	5
68. M., Deputy	5
69. Martincz de la Rosa, former Minister	5
70. Mme. Virginie Ancelot, playwright	20

	Francs
71. Louis Blanc	3
72. Mme. J. Bachellery, boarding-house owner	5
73. B., Deputy	10
74. Victor Hennequin, attorney	5
75. F. Ponsard, playwright	3
76. Mme. Desbordes-Valmore	5
77. Mme. Biberel de Saint-Germain	5
78. Resefeld, lithographer	3
79. Blaere, shoemaker	.50
80. Anonymous	2
81. Vinçard, worker	2
82. Mlle. Cécile Dufour	1
83. Mme. Anaïs Ségalas	5
84. Baroness d'Aurillac	5
85. Count de Laroche-Lambert	5
86. Anonymous	3
87. Chaales, investor	5
88. Baroness Aloyse de Carlowitz	5
89. Mlle. Sydonie de Carlowitz	3
90. A Polish lady	10
91. César Daly, architect	10
92. C., barber	1
93. P. Durand, cabinetmaker in Fontainebleau	3
94. de Chénier, attorney	5
95. Emile Souvestre, playwright	5
96. Louis Wolowski, professor of industrial law at the Conservatory	5
97. de C., Deputy	20
98. J.L.	5
99. A.C., Deputy	10
100. Tissot, French Academy	5
101. Pierre Moreau, locksmith in Auxerre	5
102. Mme. Louise Colet	5
103. Paul Renouard, printer	5
104. Auguste Barbier	10

	Francs
105. Firmin Didot, Bros., printers	10
106. A., Deputy	10
107. Lacour and Maistrasse, printers	10
108. C., landlord	10
109. Mme. Eugénie Lemaître	1.50
110. E. Barrault	10
111. G. Duprez, singer	5
112. Mme. Emélie, dressmaker	1
113. Delse Pareto, architect	25
114. Paul de Kock	1
115. P. Poultier, singer	5
116. Gustave Barba, bookseller	5
117. E. D., attorney	10
118. Anonymous	5
119. Mme. M., stockholder	2
120. Anonymous	3
121. L. Desnoyers	5
122. Marie Dorval, actress	5
123. Four students	4
Total received	1,548
Expenses: printing costs, paper, etc.	932

With all the expenses paid, 616 francs remain, as can be seen. This money will be used for postal costs, etc.

All these details may seem a bit long, but if the reader takes my very exceptional position into account, he will understand that I had to provide this explanation.

All there is to do now is to thank sincerely all the people who have been kind enough to help and honor me with their concern.

May 17, 1843   FLORA TRISTAN

NOTES

1. Cf. the life of Jean-Baptiste Languet de Gergy, Father of Saint Sulpice, in the *Biographie* by Michaud.

2. Only a few persons read the first three chapters.

TO MEN AND WOMEN
of
Faith—Love—Intelligence—Strength—Action

I would have liked to put a song summing up my idea at the beginning of my book—THE UNION, and as its refrain, "Brothers, let us unite! Sisters, let us unite!" Songs have an extraordinarily magnetic effect on gathered workers. With the help of a song, heroes ready for war or religious men ready for peace can be deliberately created.

I went straight to Béranger, everyone's poet, to ask him for the Union song.* The great poet and excellent man received me in a very brotherly manner and told me as unpretentiously as good old La Fontaine would have, "Your title is beautiful! But to make up a song in response to this title will be difficult, and I don't write songs in just any way. For that, I must wait for the inspiration . . . and I am getting old. I am not well, and in this state, inspiration does not come. But, if the song does come to me, I shall give it to the workers as the expression of my affectionate sympathy."

Then I wrote to Monsieur de Lamartine;† he replied that a *Marseillaise for peace* presented considerable problems. He ended his letter by promising me that he would think about it, and that, if he managed to come up with something satisfactory, he would send it to me for *The Workers' Union*.

I also wrote to several worker-poets in this regard. Let us hope they will respond to my appeal, that the great and beautiful notion of human fraternity will inspire them, and that they will sing of the Union.

* Pierre-Jean de Béranger (1780–1857) was an extremely popular political and patriotic songwriter, at times considered very controversial by the authorities. He also appears on Tristan's subscription list.

† Alphonse de Lamartine (1790–1869), one of the master poets of French Romanticism, was elected Deputy in 1834 and pursued a political career until 1848, putting his poetic talents to use for the liberal cause.

To Working Men and Women

Listen to me. For twenty-five years the most intelligent and devoted men have given their lives to defending your sacred cause.[1] In their writings, speeches, reports, memoirs, investigations, and statistics, they have pointed out, observed, and demonstrated to the government and the wealthy that the working class, in the current state of affairs, is morally and materially placed in an intolerable situation of poverty and grief. They have shown that, in this state of abandonment and suffering, most of the workers, inevitably embittered through misfortune and brutalized through ignorance, become dangerous to society. They have proven to the Government and the wealthy that not only justice and humanity call for the duty of aiding them through a law on labor organization, but that even the public interest and security imperiously demand such a measure. Well, for the last twenty-five years, so many eloquent voices have not been able to arouse the Government's concern regarding the risks to society with seven to eight million workers exasperated by suffering and despair, with many trapped between suicide and thievery!

Workers, what can be said now in defense of your cause? In the last twenty-five years, hasn't everything been said and repeated in every form? There is nothing more to be said, nothing more to be written, for your wretched position is well known by all. Only one thing remains to be done: *to act by virtue of the rights inscribed in the Charter.**

Now the day has come when one must *act*, and it is up to you

* The Constitutional Charter was granted by Louis XVIII in 1814 and revised in 1830 under Louis-Philippe. See Chapter II, where Tristan cites a number of articles from the 1830 Charter.

and *only* you to act in the interest of your own cause. At stake are your very lives . . . or death, that horrible, ever-menacing death: misery and starvation.

Workers, put an end to twenty-five years of waiting for someone to intervene on your behalf. Experience and facts inform you well enough that the Government cannot or will not be concerned with your lot when its improvement is at issue. It is up to you alone, if you truly want it, to leave this labyrinth of misery, suffering, and degradation in which you languish. Do you want to ensure good vocational education for your children and for yourselves, and certainty of rest in your old age? You can.

Your action is not to be armed revolt, public riots, arson, or plundering. No, because, instead of curing your ills, destruction would only make them worse. The Lyons and Paris riots have attested to that.* You have but one legal and legitimate recourse permissible before God and man: THE UNIVERSAL UNION OF WORK-ING MEN AND WOMEN.

Workers, your condition in present society is miserable and painful: in good health, you do not have the right to work; sick, ailing, injured, old, you do not even have the right to care; poor, lacking everything, you are not entitled to benefits, and beggary is forbidden by law. This precarious situation relegates you to a primitive state in which man, living in nature, must consider every morning how he will get food for the day. Such an existence is true torture. The fate of the animal ruminating in a stable is a thousand times better than yours. He, at least, is certain of eating the next day; his master keeps hay and straw for him in winter. The bee in its tree hole is a thousand times better off than you. The ant who works in summer to live well in winter is a

---

* See Translator's Introduction, pp. xii–xiii; these very serious riots spontaneously broke out in Lyons in 1831 a few weeks after a group of textile workers met unsuccessfully with a group of businessmen to agree upon a minimum wage. In 1834 there were more riots in Lyons, where in five days 1,200 deaths occurred, and some in Paris, where meetings of twenty or more persons were outlawed.

thousand times better off than you. Workers, you are miserable, yes, indubitably; but what is the main cause of your suffering? If a bee or an ant, instead of working with other bees and ants to stock the common dwelling for winter, decided to separate and work alone, it too would die of cold and hunger all alone in a corner. Then why do you remain isolated from each other? Individually, you are weak and fall from the weight of all kinds of miseries. So, leave your isolation: unite! *Unity gives strength.* You have numbers going for you, and numbers are significant.

I come to you to propose a general union among working men and women, regardless of trade, who reside in the same region— a union which would have as its goal the CONSOLIDATION OF THE WORKING CLASS and the construction of several establishments (Workers' Union palaces), distributed evenly throughout France. Children of both sexes six to eighteen would be raised there; and sick or disabled workers as well as the elderly would be admitted.[2] Listen to the numbers and you will have an idea of what can be done with the union.

In France there are about five million working-class men and two million women—seven million workers united in thought and action.[3] To realize a great, communal project for the benefit of *all* men and women, if each contributes two francs per year, at the end of one year, the Workers' Union will have the enormous sum of fourteen million francs.

You are going to say to me, "But how do we unite for this great project? Because of our job situations and rivalries, we are all dispersed and often are even enemies at war with each other. And two francs yearly is a lot for poor day workers!"*

I shall respond to these two objections: *uniting* for the accomplishment of a great project is not *associating*. Soldiers and sailors, who each contribute equally through withheld wages to a com-

---

*As noted earlier, the average worker's wage in mid-nineteenth century France was about twenty centimes per hour. Thus a fifteen-hour day would amount to one and a half francs.

mon fund to take care of 3,000 soldiers and sailors at the Hôtel des Invalides, are not *associates* for that reason. They do not need to know one another, nor have similar opinions, tastes, or personalities. All they need to know is that from one end of France to the other all the military contribute the same amount, which assures the right of admission to the hospital for the wounded, sick, and aged.

As for the amount, I ask, who among the workers, even the poorest, cannot manage to save two francs in the course of a year to assure a place for retirement in his old age?[4] Your neighbors, the unfortunate Irish and the *poorest* people on earth, the people who eat only potatoes, and then only every other day[5]—these people (numbering only seven million souls) found the means to provide about two million in income for a single man (O'Connell),[6] their defender, it is true, but for one man alone, and for twelve years! And you, the French, the *richest* on earth, you wouldn't be able to find the means to build big, sanitary, convenient palaces for your children, the injured, and the elderly? This would be truly shameful, an eternal shame to impute your selfishness, lack of caring and lack of intelligence! Yes, if the Irish workers who go barefoot and without food gave two million a year for twelve years to their defender, you French can easily give fourteen million a year to house and feed your good veterans of labor and to raise the young.

Two francs a year! Who among you does not pay ten or twenty times that for his little private trade club, welfare society, or little bad habits like tobacco, coffee, liquor, etc.? Two francs each is not hard to find[7] and, with each of you giving this little bit, a total of fourteen million can be raised. Look at what wealth you possess only by your *number*. But to enjoy that wealth, everyone must join together and create *unity*.

Workers, put aside then your petty trade rivalries and move beyond your private associations toward a compact, solid, and indissoluble Union. Tomorrow and immediately, may one and the same thought spontaneously arise from all your hearts: the Union! Let this cry for unity resound throughout France, and in a year, if you truly want it, the Union will be established, and in two years you will have fourteen million in funds of your very own to build a palace worthy of a great working people.

On the outside above the entrance, you will put in bronze letters:

WORKERS' UNION PALACE

CONSTRUCTED AND MAINTAINED THROUGH ANNUAL MEMBERSHIP OF
2 FRANCS DONATED BY WORKING MEN AND WOMEN TO HONOR WORK
AS IT DESERVES TO BE HONORED AND TO REWARD THE WORKERS,
who feed and enrich the nation and constitute its true power.
HONOR TO WORK
IN RESPECT AND GRATITUDE TO THE GOOD VETERANS OF LABOR

Yes, champions of labor, it is up to you to be the first to raise your voices in honor of the only truly honorable thing—*work*. Producers, scorned by those who exploit you, it is up to you first to build a palace for your workers' retirement. You who are builders of palaces for kings and the rich, of God's temples and asylums to shelter mankind, it is finally up to you to construct a haven where you can die in peace. Otherwise you have only the hospice, and then when there is room. So, to work, to work!

Workers, think about the effort I have just made to enable you to leave behind your misery. If you do not answer this call for unity, if through selfishness or lack of caring you refuse to unite, what can be done to save you in the future?

Brothers, striking the heart of all those who write for the people is the distressing thought that, as of a young age, the poor are so abandoned and so overworked that three-quarters of them do not know how to read and the other quarter does not have time to read. So, to write a book for the people is like throwing a drop of water into the sea. That is why I realized that limiting my plan for a Universal Union to paper, as magnificent as it is, would create a dead letter, as had happened to so many other plans previously proposed. I realized that, with my book published, I had another task to accomplish, which is to go from town to town and from one end of France to the other with my union plan in hand to speak to those workers who do not know how to read or have no time to read. I told myself that the time had come to act. And for the one who really loves the workers and wishes to devote body and soul to their cause, there is a beautiful mission to fulfill. The example given by Christ's first apostles must be followed. Defying persecution and fatigue, those men took a staff and sack and went from country to country preaching the new law—fraternity and unity in God. Well, as a woman who feels faith and force, why shouldn't I go, just like the apostles, from town to town announcing the good tidings and preaching fraternity and unity in humanity to the workers?

The workers have often been spoken *of* in the legislature, from the Christian pulpit, in society gatherings, on the stage, and especially in the courts. But no one has yet tried to speak *to* them. This had to be attempted. The Lord tells me it will succeed. That is why I am so confidently embarking on a new path. Yes, I shall go and find them in their workshops, in their attic rooms, and even in their taverns, if necessary. And amidst their very misery, I shall convince them about their own fate and force them, in spite of themselves, to escape the terror of that degrading and fatal poverty.

NOTES

1. Saint-Simon, Owen, Fourier, and their schools; Parent-Duchâtelet, Eugène Buret, Villermé, Pierre Leroux, Louis Blanc, Gustave de Beaumont, Proudhon, Cabet; and among the workers, Adolphe Boyer, Agricol Perdiguier, Pierre Moreau, etc.

2. See Chapter IV, The Procedure for Admission.

3. See the statisticians' works and the remarkable work by Pierre Leroux, *De la Ploutocratie*, for the exact numbers.

4. That makes only 17 centimes per month.

5. The Irish eat meat only *once* a year, on New Year's Day. "Being poor, they only eat the cheapest food in the country, potatoes. But they do not all eat the same amount: the privileged eat potatoes three times a day; other less fortunate ones, twice a day; and the very poor eat only once a day. There are some even more deprived who go for one or even two days without any food" (*L'Irelande sociale, politique et religieuse*, by Gustave de Beaumont, Part I, Chapter I. For greater detail, see the rest of the chapter).

6. O'Connell responded to Lord Shrewsbury, who had criticized the voluntary annual subsidy of 75,000 pounds sterling Ireland pays him. O'Connell's very stunning reply ended with these words, "I am proud to proclaim that I am the paid servant of Ireland, and it is a livery I can boast of wearing" (Session in the House of Commons, October 1842).

7. The membership fee could be paid in two installments.

I

On the
Insufficiency of
Welfare Societies, Guilds, etc.

While reading the *Book on Compagnonnage* by Agricol Perdiguier
(a cabinetmaker), a little pamphlet by Pierre Moreau (locksmith),[1]
and the "Plan to Regenerate the Guild System," by Monsieur
Gosset, master blacksmith, I was struck and enlightened by this
great idea of the *universal union of men and women workers.**

Compagnonnage is best understood as "guild system." In France,
these guilds had long histories of rivalry and were as much fraternities
as they were trade associations. The companion's apprenticeship included a "tour of France" that provided work experience, travel, and
opportunities for vocational competition with members of other guilds;
encounters between members of rival guilds often resulted in street
fighting and riots. The journal Tristan kept during her final and fatal
mission to organize the workers reported her adaptation of the French
tour.

Of the three worker-poets Tristan mentions, Agricol Perdiguier
(1805–75), whose nickname was "Virtue from Avignon," was among
the most visible and respected. Encouraged by George Sand, he wrote
several books about the "guild" existence and was elected the people's
representative to the republican government in 1848. He also served
as the fictional model for Sand's protagonist in her novel *The Companion of the Tour of France* (1851). Pierre Moreau (1811–71) had written
"Un Mot sur le compagnonnage ou le guide de l'ouvrier sur le tour de
France" in 1841, and it is the work Tristan must have read first. Her
footnote refers to his "De la Réforme des abus du compagnonnage et
de l'amélioration du sort des travailleurs" (1843). Jean Gosset, nick-
named the Father of Blacksmiths, wrote several pamphlets to express

In these three rather remarkable but small works the question of workers is envisioned by workers, intelligent and conscientious men, who are thoroughly familiar with the subject. The three works are thought out and written in good faith; ardent and sincere love for humanity can be felt on every page, precious qualities not always encountered in the learned works written by our famous economists.

After showing us the guild system as it is today, the three worker writers proposed significant reforms for the various guild groups (Moreau in particular), each according to his character and way of seeing things. These reforms could doubtless improve the workers' habits; but, I must say, what struck me was seeing that, among the improvements proposed by Messrs. Perdiguier, Moreau, and the father of blacksmiths, none was of the caliber to bring about a veritable, positive amelioration in the physical and psychological condition of the working class. In fact, let us suppose that all these reforms might be realized. Let us suppose that, according to M. Perdiguier's wish the guild members no longer fought among themselves; that according to M. Moreau's design, discrimination among trades disappeared to form a General Union; and that according to the master blacksmith's desire guild members were no longer exploited by the "mothers."* Indeed, these would be lovely results. But, I ask, how would these reforms

---

his preoccupation with regenerating the guilds. The complete title of the one Tristan read is "Projet tendant à régénérer le Compagnonnage sur le Tour de France, soumis à tous les ouvriers" (Paris, 1842).

* Perdiguier gives the following definition of the "mothers": "When a companion goes to the inn where the Society is lodged, eats and holds its meetings, he says, 'I am going to the mother's.' If the innkeeper does not have a wife, one would still say, 'I am going to the mother's.' One can see that the word 'mother' evokes not only the mistress of the house but the house itself"; see *Mémoires d'un compagnon* (Paris: Union Générale d'Editions, 1964), p. 303.

change the precarious, miserable situation of the working class? In no way, or at least very little.

I do not know how to explain why these three worker writers, who so brilliantly pointed out small, specific reforms, did not think to propose a plan for a universal union whose goal would be to put the working class in a social position to demand its right to work, its right to education, and its right to be represented before the country. For it is very clear that that is where all the other improvements would naturally come from. This very important lacuna in these three writings made a deep impression upon me. That is when I was enlightened by the great and beautiful notion of the universal union of working men and women.

In thinking about the causes of the abuses and ills of all sorts pointed out by the worker writers, I saw where the evil came from and instantly understood what remedy can be applied. Isn't poverty the true cause, the only cause of all the evils afflicting the working class?

Yes, it is poverty, and because of it, the working class is condemned forever to wallow in ignorance, degradation, and enslavement. So poverty must be fought; it is the most redoubtable enemy!

In my opinion, anyone who sincerely wants the real and effective improvement of the most *populous* and *useful* class[2] can propose only an easily and simply implemented means to give the working class the opportunity of leaving its precarious state gradually and nonviolently. And I have just proposed this means which is easy to implement and promises to be effective.

Workers, I must warn you, I shall not flatter you—I loathe flattery. My language will be frank and severe; at times you will find it a bit rough. I believe it is useful, urgent, and indispensable that one speak to you openly and frankly, without fear of insulting your pride, no matter what your faults. When one wants to heal a wound, one bares it to clean it, and then it can heal.

If I speak to you with an openness you are unaccustomed to, instead of turning me away, just listen more attentively. For you must always keep in mind that they who flatter you only intend to use you, not be of use to you.

"I tell you these truths about your faults," said Christ, "because I love you; they who flatter you do not love you."

NOTES

1. When I wrote this chapter, Monsieur P. Moreau's last work had not yet appeared.

2. I do not know why the Saint-Simonians used to say, "the most *populous* and the *poorest* class." Poverty is not a quality, far from it! I have replaced the word poverty with the word *useful*, because it is precise. And since usefulness is a precious quality, it becomes an irrefutable title for the laboring class.

II

How to Consolidate the Working Class

It is very important for the workers to distinguish between the Workers' Union as I conceive of it and what exists today under the titles of guild associations, the Union, welfare societies, etc. The goal of all these various private groups is simply to give aid, mutually and individually, within each society. Thus they were set up to provide in case of sickness, accidents, and long periods of unemployment.

Given the working class's current state of isolation, desertion, and misery, these kinds of societies serve a purpose. For their aim is to give a bit of aid to the most needy, thereby mitigating some personal suffering, which often surpasses the strength and stamina of those afflicted. So I highly approve of these societies and encourage the workers to increase them and get rid of the abuses they may have. But alleviating misery does not *destroy* it; mitigating the evil is not the same as *eradicating* it. If one really wants to attack the root of evil, obviously one needs something other than private societies, since their only goal is to relieve individual suffering.

Let us examine what happens in the private societies and see whether this mode of action can actually improve the lot of the working class. Each society uses its membership fees to give so much per diem (between 50 centimes and 2 francs) to the sick and in some cases to those who have been out of work for a certain length of time. If, by chance, something happens, such as a member's being sent to prison, aid is available up to the time of the verdict. In the guild associations mutual aid is even more effective: members obtain work for those coming from provincial towns and let the mother* know what their expenses are, up to a certain limit, while waiting for work. That is what they do on the material side. To boost their morale, each member of the association makes it his duty to go and visit sick members in their homes or in the hospital, and prisoners, as well. I repeat, given the current state of affairs, these sorts of groups are at least very useful in showing great sympathy and in binding the workers, for they encourage good morals, civilize their customs, and alleviate their awful suffering. But is that sufficient? No! Indeed not, since, in the final analysis, these groups cannot (and do not claim to) change or improve in any way the material and moral condition of the working class.

A father belonging to one of these associations suffers miserably, and finds no solace in believing that his sons will be any better off than he. And in their turn, his sons as members of the same association will live miserably like their fathers, with no hope for their children. Mind you, each society acting in the name of the individual and trying to provide temporary relief invariably offers the same thing. Despite all its efforts, it will be able to create nothing great, good, or capable of notable results.[1] Therefore, Workers, with your private societies as they have existed since the time of Solomon, the physical and pychological condition of the working class will not have changed in fifty centuries: its fate will always be poverty, ignorance, and slavery, the only change being the types and names of slaves.

* See p. 46n, for an explanation of the guild "mother."

What is wrong? This kind of absurd, selfish, mean, bastard organization divides the working class into a multitude of small private groups, the way large empires,[2] which we see today as so strong, rich, and powerful, were divided during the Middle Ages into small provinces, which in turn were further divided into small towns with their own rights and freedoms. Well, what rights! That is to say, the little towns and provinces, continually at war with each other (and today war is competition), were poor, weak, and had as their only right the ability to moan under the weight of their wretchedness, isolation, and the terrible calamities inevitably resulting from their divisive state.

So I am not afraid to repeat that the fundamental vice which must be attacked from every point is the system of separation, which decimates the workers and can only foster abuse.

I think this short analysis will suffice to enlighten the workers about the true cause of their ills—*division*.

Workers, you must leave behind this division and isolation as quickly as possible and march courageously and fraternally down the only appropriate path—*unity*. My union plan rests upon a broad base, and its spirit is capable of fully satisfying the moral and material needs of a great people.

What is the aim and what will result from the universal union of working men and women? Its goals are:

1. to establish the solid, indissoluble unity of the working class;

2. to provide the Workers' Union with great capital through the optional membership of every worker;

3. to acquire a real power backed by this capital;

4. by means of this power, to prevent poverty and eradicate abuse by giving working-class children a solid, rational education which will make them educated, reasonable, intelligent, and able men and women in their work;

5. to remunerate labor as it ought to be, generously and fairly.

"This is too beautiful!" one will cry. "It is too beautiful; so it

is *impossible.*" Readers, before surpressing your feelings and imagination with the icy words, "it is impossible," remember that
France has between 7 and 8 million workers, and with a membership of two francs each, that makes 14 million in one year; at four
francs, 28 million; at eight francs, 56 million. This is not at all
whimsical. There are some well-off workers, and above all, many
with generous souls. Some will give two francs, others four,
eight, ten or twenty. And just think of how many you are, seven
million![3]

Now let us examine the results the Worker's Union could have.
I have just shown that it is not at all impossible for seven million
workers, united in this concept, to serve their cause and their
own interests. Through voluntary contributions, they could collect 15, 20, 30, 40 or 50 million francs a year. Applied to the
gears of a huge machine like the government, 20-50 million is
hardly anything; but applied toward a specific object and used
carefully, economically, and intelligently, 20-50 million represents enormous wealth. I have stated that with this capital the
Workers' Union could acquire true power, the one money grants.
Let us see how.

For instance, the Irish with their union were able to set up and
support something called the Association.[4] Moreover, through
voluntary contributions,[5] they were able to establish a gigantic
fortune for an honorable and talented man, O'Connell. Follow
closely and you will see what can come of a union. O'Connell
became Ireland's defender. Highly paid by the people who had
mandated him, he was able to deploy both offense and defense
on a large scale. Should he judge it appropriate to publish ten,
twenty, or thirty tracts to be distributed by the thousands
throughout Ireland, he could do it, having the money at his disposal. And his agents would distribute them in all the towns.
Should he deem it important to get his son, son-in-law, or a
trusted friend into the House of Commons, he had his agents give
out guineas en masse to the voters, and the association's repre-

sentative reached the Chamber to defend Ireland's interest.* If I constantly cite Ireland, it is because Ireland is still the only country to realize that if the people want to leave their slavery, they must begin first by creating a huge, solid, and indissoluble union. For the union gives strength, and in order to demand one's rights and to bring the right of such a demand to public attention, one must above all be in a position to speak authoritatively enough to make oneself heard.

The situation of the French working class cannot be compared in any way to the cruel position of the Irish people. A conquered country whose spirit of independence refuses to be resigned to bearing the yoke of oppression, Ireland is demanding religious, political, and civil rights from its lords and masters. The very articulation of that demand proves that this unhappy people is treated like slaves, since it enjoys no rights. At least, in principle, and this is considerable, we legally have no more slaves, at least among the male population. What is the social position of the French working class today, and what rights remain to be demanded?

Theoretically, the organic law ruling French society since the Declaration of the Rights of Man in 1791 is the highest expression of justice and equity. For this law is the solemn recognition legitimizing the holiness of the principle of absolute equality, and not only that equality under God claimed by Christ, but that living equality practiced in the name of body and soul in humanity. Workers, do you want to know what your rights are in theory? Open the law book governing French society and you will see:

"Art. 1. The French people are equal before the law, regardless of their title or rank.

"Art. 2. In proportion to their wealth, they indiscriminately contribute to the State.

* It appears that buying ballots did not strike Tristan as immoral or deviously manipulative.

"Art. 3. They all have equal opportunity for civil and military employment.

"Art. 4. Their individual freedom is equally guaranteed; a person cannot be pursued or arrested except under law, in the form prescribed by law. . . .

"Art. 8. All property is inviolable not excepting any called *national*, as the law does not discriminate among them."

In fact, according to the spirit and the letter of the Charter's articles, the French worker has no claims with respect to the citizen's and man's dignity. From the Charter's standpoint, his social position is as desirable as he could want. By virtue of the recognized principle, he enjoys absolute equality, complete freedom of thought, and the guarantee of security for his person and property. What more can he ask? But, let us hasten to say that to enjoy equality and freedom *in theory* is to live *in spirit*. And if he who brought the law of the spirit to the world spoke wisely, "Man can not live by bread alone," I believe it is also wise to say, "Man does not live in spirit alone."

Reading the 1830 Charter, one is struck by a serious omission. Our constitutional legislators forgot that preceding the rights of man and the citizen, there is an imperious, imprescriptible right engendering all the others, *the right to live*. Now, for the poor worker who possesses no land, shelter, capital, absolutely nothing except his hands, the rights of man and the citizen are of no value if his right to live is not recognized first of all (and in this case they are even bitterly derisory). For the worker, the right to live is the right to *work*, the only right that can give him the possibility of eating, and thus, of living. The first of the rights that every being enjoys by being born is precisely the one they *forgot* to inscribe in the Charter. This first right has yet to be proclaimed.[6]

Today the working class must be concerned with this single claim, because it is based on the strictest equity. And anything short of granting this claim is an abrogation of fundamental rights.

So, what is to be demanded? THE RIGHT TO WORK. The working class's own property and the only one it can ever possess is its hands. Yes, its hands. That is its patrimony, its sole wealth. Its hands are the only work tools it has. Therefore they constitute its property, and I do not think its legitimacy or utility can be denied. For if the earth produces, it is thanks to manual labor.

To deny that the worker's hands are his property is to refuse to understand the spirit of Article 8 of the Charter. Yet this property is uncontestable and, as soon as it comes under discussion, there will be a unanimous voice in support of it. To guarantee the working class's property (as Art. 8 indicates), this right and its free enjoyment must be recognized in principle (as well as in reality). Now, the exercise of this free enjoyment of property would consist in being able to use its hands when and how it pleases. And for that, it must have the *right to work*. So the guarantee of this property consists in a wise and equitable *organization of labor*. The working class thus has two important demands to make: *The right to work* and *the right to organize*.

"But," it will still be said, "what you demand for the working class is impossible. The right to work! That cannot be achieved. This demand, no matter how just and legal, will be considered an attack on property per se (land, houses, capital). And labor organization will be considered an attack on the rights of private enterprise. And, since those who lead the governmental machine are land and capital owners, it is obvious they will never agree to grant such rights to the working class."

Let us understand one another. If in their current state of division and isolation the workers decide to demand the right to work and to organize, the proprietors will not even do them the honor of considering their demand an attack: they will not listen to them. A worker of merit (Adolphe Boyer) wrote a little book in which he makes both demands. No one has read his book. Out of chagrin and misery, and perhaps with the thought that his tragic end would create readers, the poor man killed himself. The press was moved for a moment, for four days, maybe eight days. Then Adolphe Boyer's suicide and little book were completely forgotten. Even if Boyer's book had been perfect, who would have read it? Who would have promoted it and made it known? What results would it have brought about? None. Boyer was a poor worker who wrote all alone in his corner. He defended his unhappy brothers' cause, that is true; but he was not tied to them in thought, feeling, or interest. So he killed himself because he did not have the 200 francs to pay for the costs incurred by his little book. Do you think that would have happened if Boyer had belonged to a big union? No, probably not. First of all, the union would have paid the costs of the book; then the book would have been read; the value of his plan would have been discussed. Seeing that his work was appreciated and that his ideas could be useful, Boyer would have felt great satisfaction. And encouraged by his brothers, Boyer would have continued to work for the cause, instead of committing suicide out of despair. See the difference in results! When the workers are divided, Boyer, a man of heart, intelligence, and talent, is forced to kill himself because he wrote a book. Had they been united, this same man would have lived a fulfilled and respected life, working valiantly for the very same reason—because he would have written a book.

Workers, you see, if you want to save yourselves, you have but one means, you must unite. If I preach unity, it is because I know the strength and power you will find. Open your eyes, look around you, and you will see the advantages enjoyed by all those who have created unity in the goal of serving a common cause and common interests.

Notice how all intelligent men have proceeded: for example, founders of religions. The first thing they were concerned with was establishing the union. Moses united his people with such strong ties that even time cannot tear them apart. Jerusalem fell; the temple was razed; the Jewish nation was destroyed; the people of Moses wandered aimlessly on earth. No matter! Every

Jew, at the bottom of his heart, feels united in thought with his brothers. Thus, you see, the Jewish nation did not die, and after 2,000 years of unparalleled persecution and misery, the Jewish people are still standing! What did Christ do before his death? He gathered his twelve apostles and united them in his name and through communion. The master died. No matter! Unity was consolidated. Since then the master's spirit has lived on in unity. And while this redoubtable man, whose energetic protest frightened the power of the Caesars, died on the cross, in Jerusalem and in all the towns of Judea, Jesus Christ survived in his apostles and in eternal life. For after John, Peter was born, and after Peter, Paul was born, and so on until the end of time. Twelve united men established the Catholic church,[7] a huge union which became so powerful that one can say it has governed most of the world for two thousand years.

On a smaller scale, see the same principle of strength repeated: Luther, Calvin, and all the Catholic dissidents. As soon as they form a union, they become powerful.

Now, to another domain. The Revolution of 1789 breaks out. Like a torrent devastating everything in its path, it upsets, exiles, and slays. But the Royalist union is established. Even overwhelmed by numbers, it is so strong that it survives the Terror of 1793, and twenty years later, it returns to France with its king at its head. And before such results you stubbornly stay isolated! No, you can do so no longer—to persist would be madness.

In 1789 the bourgeoisie gained its independence. Its own charter dates from the capture of the Bastille. Workers, for more than two hundred years the bourgeois have fought courageously and ardently against the privileges of the nobility and for the victory of their rights.[8] But when the day of victory came, and though they recognized *de facto* equal rights for all, they seized all the gains and advantages of the conquest for themselves alone.

The bourgeois class has been established since 1789. Note what strength a body united in the same interest can have. As soon as this class is recognized, it becomes so powerful that it can exclusively take over all the country's powers. Finally in 1830 its power reaches its peak, and without being the least bit troubled by what might occur, it pronounces the fall of France's reigning king. It chooses its own king, proceeds to elect him without consulting the rest of the nation, and finally, being actually sovereign, it takes the lead in business and governs the country as it pleases. This bourgeois-owners class represents itself in the legislature and before the nation, not to defend its own interests, for no one threatens them, but to impose its conditions and commands upon 25 million proletarians. In a word, it is both counsel and judge, just like the feudal lords it triumphed over. Being capitalists, the bourgeois make laws with regard to the commodities they have to sell, and thereby regulate, as they will, the prices of wine, meat, and even the people's bread. You see, already more numerous and useful, the bourgeoisie has succeeded the nobility. The unification of the working class now remains to be accomplished. In turn, the workers, the vital part of the nation, must create a huge union to assert their unity! Then, the working class will be strong; then it will be able to make itself heard, to demand from the bourgeois gentlemen its right to work and to organize.

The advantage all large constitutional bodies enjoy is the ability to count for something in the State, and in this way, be represented. Today, the Royalist union has its representative in the Chamber, with its delegate before the nation to defend its interest, its defender being the most eloquent man in France— Monsieur Berryer.* The colonial union has its representatives in the Chamber, with its delegates before the motherland to defend its interest. Well, once assembled in body, why wouldn't the working class have its representative before the legislature and nation to defend *its* interests? Indeed, in number and importance,

* Antoine Berryer (1790–1868), a lawyer and orator who later opposed the Second Empire.

it equals at least the Royalist group and the body of colonial landowners.

Workers, think about this: the first thing you have to do is to get yourselves represented before the nation.

I stated above that the Workers' Union would enjoy real power, that of money. In fact, it will be easy to allocate 500,000 francs a year out of 20 or 30 million to support generously a defender worthy of serving the cause. We cannot doubt that in beautiful, generous, chivalrous France, men of O'Connell's dedication and talent will be found. So if the Workers' Union is well aware of its position and true interests, its first act must be a solemn appeal to men who feel enough love, strength, courage, and talent to dare take on the defense of the most sacred of causes—the workers'.

Who knows yet what France has in the way of generous hearts and capable men? Who can foresee the effect produced by an appeal made in the name of seven million workers demanding the right to work? Poor, isolated workers, you count for nothing in the nation. But as soon as the Workers' Union is established, the working class will become a powerful and respectable body; and men of the highest merit will court the honor of being chosen to defend it.

Should the Union be formed in the near future, let us take a quick look at the men who have shown sympathy for the working class, and see who would be the most capable of serving this sacred cause. Let us adopt a humanitarian point of view, and since we are looking for men of love and intelligence, let us not consider their religious and political opinions. Besides, the Union's trustee need not be concerned with either political or religious questions. His mission will be limited to drawing public attention to two points: the right to work and labor organization for everyone's well-being.

Since the rise of Napoleon, France has had illustrious generals, distinguished scientists, and talented artists, but *very few* men devoted to the people or aware of how to serve them effectively. Today, just a few names stand out.

Gustave de Beaumont: in writing his beautiful work on Ireland, he has shown great love for the poor. Great courage was necessary to probe such awful and repugnant wounds. Endowed with great intelligence, Monsieur de Beaumont quickly recognized the cause, and indicated the necessary remedy: "The right to work or charity must be granted to the poor and one must finally think about organizing labor."

Louis Blanc: not claiming absolutely the right to work for everyone, he does certainly approve of the soundness of this demand. Moreover, he thinks he has found the means to organize labor. We shall not discuss the merit of his plan here; it is his idea and would remain outside his mandate. These are his credentials: Louis Blanc has been devoted to the defense of the people's interests since his youth. In all his work and through his concern for mankind's happiness, he has always warmly and passionately demanded rights for the most populous and useful class. Finally, in his work on labor organization, he has boldly pointed out the people's suffering and has also indicated the absolute necessity of labor organization as a remedy.

Prosper Enfantin: to many, this name inspires great dislike. However, justice must be rendered to each, which means making known the good and the bad about a person. As the leader of a school, what has Enfantin done? He did commit some serious errors. It can even be said that he, Saint-Simon's premier disciple, destroyed and annihilated forever the Saint-Simonian school which attracted such remarkable men and which had such advanced views on all the social issues. But besides those really disastrous and irreparable faults, it must be recognized that Monsieur Enfantin has given a great example as the first to try to realize Saint-Simon's precept. And he also proclaimed, as the fundamental law of the Saint-Simonian doctrine, the rehabilitation and sacredness of manual labor. This rehabilitation alone contains society's radical transformation. Manual labor has always been and is still looked down upon. The only opinion in this regard is to consider manual labor degrading, shameful, and almost dishonorable for the one engaged in it.[9] This is so true that the worker hides his laboring situation as much as he can, because he himself is humiliated. He who works with his hands sees himself disdainfully cast aside everywhere; this prejudice has infiltrated the customs of all peoples and is even found in their languages. Well, it must be agreed that in face of such a state of things, Enfantin has shown great strength and superiority in teaching his disciples to honor manual labor. After establishing the law, he wanted to enforce it. So with the superior authority vested in him by his title of religious leader, he required his disciples to work with their hands, to mix among the workers, and to join them in the roughest and most repulsive trades. It seems to me that acts of this importance reveal Enfantin to have at least great energy of character and the ability to attract a lot of attention.[10]

   Still another man is crying out for the right to work and for labor organization: unlike Monsieur Beaumont or Louis Blanc, this one does not speak in the name of Christian charity or republican freedom. No, he claims a more solid foundation. It is in the name of science, and a so-called exact science (mathematics) that Victor Considérant, Fourier's foremost disciple, head of the Societarian school, distinguished author, editor-in-chief of the review *La Phalange*, demands the right to work and to organize as the *only* means left to society for salvation. Considérant possesses a science through which he believes he can *harmonically* organize our whole globe. And to produce such beautiful results, mind you, he claims it necessary to begin by organizing labor and granting everyone the right to work.[11] So here is the head of the Societarian school, a man of the highest intelligence, who calls for labor organization as the sole and complete means to regenerate society. Victor Considérant's titles are different from those of the men mentioned above. This man of science proceeds from his science and not from his heart. Nevertheless, he could offer some great advantages. Considérant is active; he speaks with spirit and great scientific conviction; and he writes the same way. And he is at the head of a school including men of merit whom he can influence. Moreover, he has been able to position himself to be heard by men in government. If Considérant were chosen by the Union, he would acquire considerable importance, which would put him in a position to serve powerfully the interests of the sacred cause.[12]

Now let us consider a very delicate matter—the size of the fee the Workers' Union should pay its defender.

Given the importance of the goal, I think it in the interest of the Workers' Union to pay him very generously; for example, 200,000, 300,000, or maybe even 500,000 francs a year. "But," it will be objected, "do you think there is a man in France who would dare accept such a huge amount taken from the small voluntary contributions made by the poor workers? Wouldn't he be afraid of being accused, like O'Connell, of selling his dedication to people?"

It is understandable that O'Connell's political enemies should adopt the tactic of heaping reproaches, insults, and slander upon him over the wages he receives from Ireland. Motivated by partisan hatred, the British aristocracy would like to defame O'Connell in the minds of the Irish to rid Ireland of its defender. Yet O'Connell's behavior is nothing but very loyal, legal, and in complete conformity with the rules established by a healthy morality.

You workers who earn a living by the sweat of your brow, don't you understand that all work deserves pay? Why shouldn't O'Connell, who works to bring Ireland out of slavery, receive the salary earned by his work? And what hard labor it is when a man gives his whole life to the defense of the popular cause! No more repose for him, as he is constantly preoccupied with seeking means of defense; day and night, he is always at work. What about the two million he receives? Can the life of the heart, the soul, and the mind be paid in gold? It is about time to remunerate services according to their usefulness.

Workers, do you know why O'Connell is slandered and why your defender will be too? I am going to tell you: because the governing aristocracy does not want the proletarian class to form a compact, solid, indissoluble union. It does not want men of merit to become the avowed and paid defenders of the working class. That is why the aristocracy, which shows great cleverness when watching over the safekeeping of its own privileges, hurls accusations of greediness and lack of scruples upon the men who dare embrace the noble defense.

But the fear of being dismissed as an impostor will, of course, not stop the truly superior man who will sense the faith and force within himself. Besides, the position of trustee for the Worker's Union will be completely different from O'Connell's. He offered his services to Ireland whereas the Workers' Union will *appeal* to the country for a defender; it will choose him and define his fee. He will only have to accept and worthily fulfill his mandate.

"How much are you going to allocate for the defender?" some will ask. "Don't you think that a man who really loves the workers' cause would defend it as well for a salary of 25 or 30,000 francs?" Workers, note that your defender's position will be rather exceptional. The defense of your cause, however sacred it may be, is not easy. Do not fool yourselves: to obtain first the right to work and then to organize, it will be necessary to fight long and hard. If you want your defender to make himself heard, place him right away in a position to acquire great power. Now, in order to achieve power in our day and age, publicity is needed; and publicity in all its forms requires money, a lot of money. If you give him 25,000 francs, what will happen? His hands will be tied, as they say, and he will not be able to act as he judges necessary. Think of how he will need to have recourse to all means of publicity, through writing (printing costs), through the writing of others (commissions), through the press (advertising costs), through trips to all the towns in France (travel expenses), through the arts (drawing, engraving, lithography costs, etc.), through entertaining society (domestic expenses), and finally propagation by all ways possible: expenses of all kinds.[13]

Think of how your defender, besides all his other qualities, must be a *clever* man. He will tactfully have to seize every means available to him to enlist supporters; and to be able to do so intelligently and on a large scale, he will need a lot of money. To maintain his property above suspicion, at the end of each year the defender will account to the central committee for his use of funds; and if it is discovered that he has spent in his private interest, his mandate will be revoked.

I emphasize this matter of a defender because I want the workers to understand thoroughly the importance to be placed on getting the Workers' Union *represented* before the country. As to the other results the Workers' Union ought to achieve, I shall not enumerate them here, because they will naturally find their place in Chapter IV.

NOTES

1. Since the advent of Christianity, there have always been in Christian lands so-called charitable societies, whose goal was to alleviate individual suffering among the poor. Well, despite the good intentions of these societies, the poor have always remained just as poor. In England, where they are literally starving to death, there are however an infinite number of charitable societies. Moreover, forced charity—the poor tax—brings in from two to three hundred million per year, excluding Scotland and Ireland (England has twelve million inhabitants). The poor tax increases every year. So, working-class poverty increases on a much larger scale.

2. To date, France, England, Russia, Austria, and the United States are the only ones unified.

3. As I have conceived of it, the Workers' Union would have as its goal first to consolidate the working class, and as an ulterior aim, to rally the 25 million *non-owner* workers from all walks of life in France to defend their interests and to demand their rights. The working class is not the only one to have to suffer from the privileges of property: artists, teachers, employees, small businessmen, and many others, even small investors who own no property such as land, houses, or capital, are fatally subjected to the laws passed by the landowners sitting in the legislature. Therefore, we cannot doubt that, as soon as the truly superior class (the dominant one in its abilities and talents, though refused a seat in the Chamber by the landowners) understands how important it is to be linked in interest and sympathy to the working class, the 25 million non-owners will of course unite their efforts to eradicate privilege. And in this aim, all will contribute more or less, as they will view the results to be obtained by the Workers' Union. Then, assuming the cooperation of the 25 million non-owners, the sum of contributions could amount to 100 million or more per year instead of the 14, 28, or 56 million francs contributed by 7 to 8 million workers.

4. The name of the Irish association has often been changed: each time it is dissolved by the Government it is immediately reformed under a new name. It has been called *United Irish, Catholic Association, General Association of Ireland, Precursors Society*. But under these various appellations, the same spirit always directs it. Here is what Monsieur de Beaumont has to say about it: "One of the particularities of the association is not only that it watches over the Government but it governs itself. It is not limited to controlling power, it exercises power. It establishes schools and charitable organizations, levies taxes to support them, protects commerce, aids industry, and does a thousand other things. For, as its powers are not defined anywhere, its limit is not delineated.

"In truth, the association is a government within the Government: a young and robust authority, born amidst a decrepit and moribund, but centralized authority which crushes and reduces

to dust all the small dispersed powers of an anti-national aristocracy" (*L'Irlande sociale, politique et religieuse*, Vol. II, p. 21).

5. They accept anything from a farthing upwards.

6. The national Convention almost recognized the right to work
or at least public assistance. The Charter makes no mention of it:
"Art. 21. Public assistance is a sacred duty. Society owes subsistence to its unfortunate citizens, either in form of providing work
or by assuring them the means to exist if they are unable to work"
(*Declaration of the Rights of Man*, June 27, 1793).

7. The term *Catholic church* means *Universal Association*.

8. In truth, if the bourgeois represented the *head*, they had the
people as *arms*, and made very good use of them too. As for you,
the workers, you have no one to help you. So you must be the
head as well as arms.

9. So that the workers do not think I am writing poetry or
imaginary works, I am going to reproduce part of a very curious
trial which can be read in its entirety in the July 7, 1841, issue of
the *Gazette des Tribunaux*. They will see how, in our day and age,
manual labor is appreciated, and in open court too!

CIVIL COURT OF THE SEINE (Fourth Chamber)
(Monsieur Michelin presiding)
Hearings on June 27 and July 6
ROBERT OWEN'S DOCTRINES. NEW HARMONY. UTILITARIAN
EDUCATION.

Atty. Durant-Saint-Amand, lawyer for Monsieur Phiquepal d'Arusmont, states the facts of this singular case in this
manner:

"The Baron de Beauséjour, Deputy and friend of General
Lafayette, whose progressive opinions he shared, had a
nephew for whom he was the guardian and whom he wanted
to give a solid education. He entrusted him to the charge of
Monsieur Phiquepal d'Arusmont and agreed to pay him an
annual sum of 1,200 francs.

"M. Phiquepal, who had been a teacher for a long time,
had enthusiastically embraced the doctrines of the famous

Scottish reformer Robert Owen, and M. de Beauséjour was aware of this.

"Robert Owen had founded an agricultural organization for the young in New Lanark, which had greatly developed and had justly brought him fame. This philosopher soon thought of enlarging his system; he resolved to do it on more land which he sought in America.

"Admitted to the national congress, he explained his plan: his methods were received, applauded, and encouraged, and he obtained a concession of land in New Harmony, where he founded a new institution under the name of Cooperative Society.

"M. Phiquepal, full of the same ideas, had formed a similar project for France; but innumerable difficulties, especially from the University, which does not allow one to break its rigid monopoly, blocked him. So he turned to America, and, after obtaining his students' and their parents' approval, he left with the former for the New World.

"After an easy crossing, M. Phiquepal and his pupils arrived in New Harmony, located in Indiana, on the banks of the Wabash, one of the large rivers in North America. Robert Owen had acquired 30,000 acres of land, partially cultivated and including a large village capable of lodging 2,000 souls. There he fervently pursued a beautiful experiment to which he had devoted both his life and fortune of several million. Above the main building, this inscription, perhaps a little pompous, could be read: *Hall of Science, Palace of Science*. Owen spread his doctrines by means of a journal called the *Free Enquirer*, which he edited with the help of his pupils.

"Such then was the place where Mr. Phiquepal had taken his pupils; such then were the masters under whom the young Dufour was to get an education. Though it would not resemble the one he would have received in Europe, it was no less apt to make him a man, as witnessed by the Baron de Beauséjour in his letters."

Here the attorney analyzes the correspondence between the Baron and his ward and concludes that the first was perfectly aware of what was happening in New Harmony and of the kind of studies his nephew was being subjected to, without ever showing any dissatisfaction.

"However, M. Phiquepal, judging it necessary to return to France, temporarily left New Harmony, leaving his pupils in the care of Owen's son. He brought with him Miss Frances Wright, whom he had decided to marry. They arrived on the Continent toward the end of 1830, and their planned union was consecrated in the presence of General Lafayette.

"At this time, the Baron de Beauséjour's ideas took a different turn. He wanted to have his nephew near him and called him back around the month of July 1831. Moreover, he warmly welcomed M. and Mme. Phiquepal and pledged them 7,200 francs in back pay.

"Back in France, the young Dufour finished his education at Monsieur Blanqui's commercial institute, and today he earns 6,000 francs a year working for the printer Everat.

"However, when the payment was due the tutor, the Baron de Beauséjour refused to pay, and numerous steps and powerful intermediaries were unable to overturn his refusal. M. Phiquepal then found himself in the painful necessity of going to court, as did the nephew. The latter was not content with denying the main contention; he counter-sued Phiquepal for 25,000 francs for damages and interest because of the *insufficiency and defectiveness of his education*. It will doubtless be curious to hear how he will try to justify this claim."

Beginning the discussion, the lawyer maintains that M. de Beauséjour knew perfectly well that the instruction given his nephew was all agricultural; that he knew what kinds of assignments he received; that he had been told his nephew knew better how to build a cabin and skipper a boat than to discourse in Greek or Latin; and being informed of all these facts when he pledged the payment of 7,200 francs, he cannot refuse to pay today.

As for Amédée Dufour's counter-suit, it is refutable by the very position he is in at the moment. If he is able to fill it, to a great extent he owes that to the education he received at the colony of new Harmony.

Atty. Flandin, in the interest of the Baron de Beauséjour, is fighting the principal claim. In a rapid discussion, he establishes that M. Phiquepal did not in any way fulfill his assignment. Instead of feeding his pupil's mind with arts and sciences, he made him into a savage, a real Indian. M. de Beauséjour does not think he has to thank him for that, on the contrary.

"As to the IOU for 7,200 francs, when he provisionally wrote it, M. de Beauséjour had not received his nephew. He was unaware of what had taken place in New Harmony. Satisfied to see Amédée involved in a voyage which, if well conducted, could become quite profitable, he was far from believing that they would take him 900 leagues away into the midst of a primitive colony. Given the country's resources and customs, his upkeep must have cost very little. It would therefore be appropriate, in any case, to reduce significantly M. Phiquepal's claim."

Atty. Sudre in his turn takes the stand for the young Dufour: "As soon as the pupils were settled, M. Phiquepal resumed their education but totally changed its objective; he subjected them to the crudest of tasks. Their duties consisted of field work, the forge, masonry, making their clothes and preparing their food; all the rest was neglected and abandoned. As for food, it was light; a little boiled corn made into bread was their usual fare, to which some game was added on Sunday when the hunt was good.

"Two years later, a new chore was added to fill Phiquepal's pupils' time. Owen junior edited the paper for the new doctrine. Called *New Harmony Gazette*, it had been handled by a printer who left the colony and was replaced by Phiquepal's pupils."

Here is a paragraph from one of Amédée Dufour's letters which shows that before seeing his uncle again he was able to appreciate the education he had received from M. Phiquepal:

"We are now staying in New York along a pretty river,

five miles from the city in the same house with Mr. Owen and Miss Wright. You must know them, at least by reputation; they edit a highly regarded paper which we print, my friends and I. I am beginning to get to know all the aspects of this fine art fairly well. I am told that I write English without many mistakes. I hope to be equally well trained in French next summer, when we shall have the opportunity of printing in that language. Besides, we have learned many little things which can, I think, help make us independent in any position we might be in. I wouldn't have trouble making shoes, clothes, my cap, bread, food, soap, butter, candles, or brooms; in a word, everything useful in a household; grow a garden, work a farm, build a cabin, a boat, and swim to safety if need be. And this helped me recently when our boat capsized in a gale; we were able to save M. Phiquepal and ourselves without much trouble."

"As soon as M. de Beauséjour was informed of all these things, he tried to clarify his nephew's lack of experience with regard to the kind of education he had been given and called him back to France. [Atty. Sudre seems to be the one quoted here.—*Trans.*]

"But young Dufour's presence soon dissipated his uncle's illusions. So-called education, the study of ancient and modern languages and the study of science, had been almost forgotten; he had to place the young man with Monsieur Blanqui, where he stayed for three years to learn the essential and truly useful things for the career his uncle intended for him.

"So it is conceivable why M. de Beauséjour now refuses to pay the 7,200 francs; it is also understandable that Amédée Dufour has a right to claim damages and interest which will always be less than the harm caused him by the deficient nature of his education."

Monsieur Bourgoin, deputy prosecutor, analyzes the facts of the case and the parties' means. He compares the task entrusted to M. Phiquepal with the education his pupils received, and concludes that the teaching completely erred from its objective.

"The Baron de Beauséjour," states the government lawyer, "had turned his nephew over to M. Phiquepal to make him a man. That was not asking too much. Well, he did not even make a man of him, but a shoemaker, a laborer, a mason, as if he belonged to one of *those* classes, in which the trowel, the jointer, or the plane is hereditary. And he neglected the very essential study of the arts, sciences, letters, modern and dead languages (if languages that have immortalized so many illustrious personages can be called that!)."

—Thus, there you have the government lawyer, the *representative of society*, declaring that shoemakers, laborers, masons ARE NOT MEN.

10. When I wrote this about Monsieur Enfantin, I was unaware that he was going to publish a book treating the question of labor organization again. The opinion stated here concerning Enfantin refers then only to what he publicly professed and had his disciples do in 1830–32. Since then, he had not said or written anything. Now M. Enfantin is reappearing on the scene as an economist, an organizer and founder. Of course, I had to get to know his new work so as to be assured that, after twelve years, the former Saint-Simonian leader had remained the defender of the most populous class (the proletariat) and the most oppressed class (women). I am finishing the book M. Enfantin has just published (*La Colonisation de l'Algérie*); I confess that my surprise was great and my sorrow deep to see how, in 1843, twelve years after the rue Monsigny meetings, Enfantin conceives of labor organization. Will it be believed? Today, for Enfantin, labor organization simply means *regimenting* the workers in a regular manner. In his mind the term *labor organization* has the same meaning as military organization. Such a way of seeing is truly beyond words! May the Lord keep you, workers, from that kind of organization. Let the most populous class perish from misery and hunger before agreeing to be regimented, which means exchanging its freedom for assurance of rations.

Monsieur Enfantin's theories, which are supposed to serve as a basis for the establishment of a new social order, are very alarming for the preservation of our freedoms, so dearly won. But we must be reassured by the fact that his doctrines on regimentation are an anachronism dating back two thousand years. Since the coming of Christ, it has no longer been possible to establish absolute dominion in the very incarnation of despotism, to require passive obedience, or to permanently jeopardize man's freedom. Kings, emperors, all those who have tried, have failed. Jesus was the first to proclaim the rights of man! And in 1791 the National Assembly ratified that sacred proclamation.

In truth, it is inconceivable that today there are people who calmly and very seriously propose to regiment men, women, and children. Such proposals are so impossible to implement that they are necessarily absurd and can only emanate from minds afflicted by monomania. After publishing such a book, Monsieur Enfantin obviously can no longer be counted on to defend the rights and liberties of the working class.

11. See *Les Destinées sociales* and *La Démocratie Pacifique*, works by Fourier and the Societarian School.

12. Other than the men I have mentioned, there are some who have shown great sympathy for the working class, for instance Pierre Leroux, Jean Reynaud, Olinde Rodrigues, Pecqueur, Lamartine, Hippolyte Carnot, Schutzenberger, Cormenin, Lamennais, Ledru-Rollin, etc.

13. As soon as a new idea or proposal appears, the essentially predictable crowd rises against it. In Britain, where O'Connell was the people's defender for fifteen years, one is beginning to understand that it is *right* and even *indispensable* for the man who devotes all his time, all his faculties, and his whole life to the defense of the people to receive enough for him and his family to live on. Thus I am only proposing for France what already exists for our neighbors.

I stated that it would be necessary to give 500,000 francs to the defender to subsidize the expenses needed to accomplish his mission. The central committee could probably reserve the right to allocate the funds requested by the defender. But as he could be refused, it might happen that the defender would cease being responsible for the movement and would be right to blame the central committee for any lags the cause might suffer. It must be understood that it is extremely important that total responsibility rest on the single head of the defender.

Thus, the establishment of the Workers' Union is tied to the defender's salary, for it makes it known to all that it is assembled as a *body* and that the body is powerful and rich enough to vest its mandate in an honorable man, by the simple fact that the working class has elected and paid a defender.

Following what I said in the text, this long note is completely useless for three-quarters of our readers, but when one must fight against the biases and suspicions of some and the scruples of others, one cannot provide too much explanation.

III
Why I Mention Women

Workers, you my brothers, for whom I work with love, because you represent the most vital, numerous, and useful part of humanity, and because from that point of view I find my own satisfaction in serving your cause, I beg you earnestly to read this with the greatest attention. For, you must be persuaded, it concerns your material interests to understand why when I mention women I always designate them as *female workers* or *all the women*.

The intelligent person enlightened by rays of divine love and love for humanity, can easily grasp the logical chain of relationships that exist between causes and effects. For him, all of philosophy and religion can be summed up by two questions: First, how can and must one love God and serve Him for the universal well-being of all men and women? Second, how can and must one love and treat woman, for the sake of all men and women? Asked in this manner, these two questions, with respect to natural order, underlie everything produced in the moral and physical worlds (one results or flows from the other).

I don't believe this is the place to answer these two questions. Later, if the workers wish it, I shall gladly treat metaphysically and philosophically questions of the highest order. But, for the time being, one need only pose the questions, as the formal declaration of an absolute principle. Without going directly back to causes, let us limit our analysis to the effects.

Up to now, woman has counted for nothing in human society. What has been the result of this? That the priest, the lawmaker, and the philosopher have treated her as a true *pariah*. Woman (one half of humanity) has been cast out of the Church, out of the law, out of society.[1] For her, there are no functions in the Church, no representation before the law, no functions in the State. The priest told her, "Woman, you are temptation, sin, and evil; you represent flesh, that is, corruption and rottenness. Weep for your condition, throw ashes on your head, seek refuge in a cloister, and mortify your heart, which is made for love, and your female organs, which are made for motherhood. And when thus you have mutilated your heart and body, offer them all bloody and dried up to your God for remission from the original sin committed by your mother Eve." Then the lawmaker tells her, "Woman, by yourself you are nothing; you have no active role in human affairs; you cannot expect to find a seat at the social banquet. If you want to live, you must serve as an appendage to your lord and master, man. So, young girl, you will obey your father; when married you shall obey your husband; widowed and old, you will be left alone." Then, the learned philosopher tells her, "Woman, it has been scientifically observed that, according to your constitution, you are inferior to man.[2] Now, you have no intelligence, no comprehension for lofty questions, no logic in ideas, no ability for the so-called exact sciences, no aptitude for serious endeavors. Finally, you are a feeble-minded and weak-bodied being, cowardly, superstitious; in a word, you are nothing but a capricious child, spontaneous, frivolous, for ten or fifteen years of your life you are a nice little doll, but full of faults and vices. That is why, woman, man must be your master and have complete authority over you."[3]

So that is how for the six thousand years the world has existed, the wisest among the wise have judged the female race.

Such a terrible condemnation, repeated for six thousand years, is likely to impress the masses, for the sanction of time has great authority over them. However, what must make us hope that this sentence can be repealed is that the wisest of the wise have also for six thousand years pronounced a no less horrible verdict upon another race of humanity—the proletariat. Before 1789, what was the proletarian in French society? A serf, a peasant, who was made into a taxable, drudging beast of burden. Then came the Revolution of 1789, and all of a sudden the wisest of the wise proclaimed that the lower orders are to be called the *people*, that the serfs and peasants are to be called *citizens*. Finally, they proclaimed the *rights of man* in full national assembly.[4]

The proletarian, considered until then a brute, was quite surprised to learn that it had been the neglect and scorn for his rights that had caused all the world's misfortunes. He was quite surprised to learn that he would enjoy civil, political, and social rights, and finally would become the *equal* of his former lord and master. His surprise grew when he was told that he possessed a brain of the same quality as the royal prince's. What a change! However, it did not take long to realize that this second judgment on the proletariat was truer than the first. Hardly had they proclaimed that proletarians were capable of all kinds of civil, military, and social functions, than out of their ranks came generals the likes of which Charlemagne, Henri IV, and Louis XIV could not recruit from the ranks of their proud and brilliant nobility.[5] Then, as if by magic, from the ranks of the proletariat surged learned men, artists, poets, writers, statesmen, and financiers who gave France a luster she had never had. Then military glory came upon her like a halo; scientific discoveries enriched her; the arts embellished her; her commerce made immense strides, and in less than thirty years the wealth of the country trebled. These facts cannot be disputed: everyone agrees today that men are born indistinct, with essentially equal faculties, and that the sole thing we should be concerned about is how to develop an individual's total faculties for the sake of the general well-being.

What happened to the proletariat, it must be agreed, is a good omen for women when their "1789" rings out. According to a very simple calculation, it is obvious that wealth will increase immeasurably on the day women are called upon to participate with their intelligence, strength, and ability in the social process. This is as easy to understand as two is the double of one. But, alas! We are not yet there. Meanwhile, let us take a look at what is happening in 1843.

The Church having said that woman was sin; the lawmaker that by herself she was nothing, that she was to enjoy no rights; the learned philosopher that by her constitution she had no intellect, it was concluded that she is a poor being disinherited by God; so men and society treated her as such.

Once woman's inferiority was proclaimed and postulated, notice what disastrous consequences resulted for the universal well-being of all men and women.

Those who believed that woman by nature lacked the strength, intelligence, and capacity to do serious and useful work, very logically deduced that it would be a waste of time to give her a rational, solid, and strict education, the kind that would make her a useful member of society. So she has been raised to be a nice doll and a slave destined for amusing and serving her master. In truth, from time to time some intelligent, sensitive men, showing empathy with their mothers, wives, and daughters, have cried out against the barbarity and absurdity of such an order of things, energetically protesting against such an iniquitous condemnation.[6] On several occasions, society has been moved for a moment; but when pushed by logic, has replied, "Well then! Let us suppose that women are not what the wise men have believed, that they have great moral strength and intelligence. Well, in that case, what good would it be to develop their faculties, since they would not be able to employ them usefully in this society which rejects them? What an awful torture, to feel one has force and power to act, and to see oneself condemned to inaction!"

This reasoning was irrefutably true. So everyone repeated,

"It's true, women would suffer too much if their God-given talents were developed, if from childhood on they were raised to understand their dignity and to be conscious of their value as members of society. Then never would they be able to bear the degradation imposed upon them by the Church, the law, and prejudice. It is better to treat them like children and leave them in the dark about themselves: they will suffer less."

Follow closely, and you will see what horrible consequences result from accepting a false premise.

In order not to stray too far from my subject, even though it is a good opportunity to speak from a general standpoint, I am returning to the question of the working class.

In the life of the workers, woman is everything. She is their sole providence. If she is gone, they lack everything. So they say, "It is woman who makes or unmakes the home," and this is the clear truth: that is why it has become a proverb. However, what education, instruction, direction, moral or physical development does the working-class woman receive? None. As a child, she is left to the mercy of a mother and grandmother who also have received no education. One of them might have a brutal and wicked disposition and beat and mistreat her for no reason; the other might be weak and uncaring, and let her do anything. (As with everything I am suggesting, I am speaking in general terms; of course, there are numerous exceptions.) The poor child will be raised among the most shocking contradictions—hurt by unfair blows and treatment one day, then pampered and spoiled no less perniciously the next.

Instead of being sent to school,[7] she is kept at home in deference to her brothers and so that she can share in the housework, rock the baby, run errands, or watch the soup, etc. At the age of twelve she is made an apprentice. There she continues to be exploited by her mistress and often continues to be as mistreated as she was at home.

Nothing embitters the character, hardens the heart, or makes the spirit so mean as the continuous suffering a child endures from unfair and brutal treatment. First, the injustice hurts, afflicts, and causes despair; then when it persists, it irritates and exasperates us and finally, dreaming only of revenge, we end up by becoming hardened, unjust, and wicked. Such will be the normal condition for a poor girl of twenty. Then she will marry, without love, simply because one must marry in order to get out from under parental tyranny. What will happen? I suppose she will have children, and she, in turn, will be unable to raise them suitably. She will be just as brutal to them as her mother and grandmother were to her.[8]

Working class women, take note, I beg you, that by mentioning your ignorance and incapacity to raise your children, I have no intention in the least of accusing *you* or *your nature*. No, I am accusing society for leaving you uneducated—you, women and mothers, who actually need so much to be instructed and formed in order to be able to instruct and develop the men and children entrusted to your care.

Generally women of the masses are brutal, mean, and sometimes hard. This being true, where does this situation come from, so different from the sweet, good, sensitive, and generous nature of woman?

Poor working women! They have so many reasons to be irritated! First, their husbands. (It must be agreed that there are few working-class couples who are happily married.) Having received more instruction, being the head by law and also by the money he brings home,[9] the husband thinks he is (and he is, in fact) very superior to his wife, who only brings home her small daily wage and is merely a very humble servant in her home.

Consequently, the husband treats his wife with nothing less than great disdain. Humiliated by his every word or glance, the poor woman either openly or silently revolts, depending upon her personality. This creates violent, painful scenes that end up producing an atmosphere of constant irritation between the master and the slave (one can indeed say *slave*, because the woman is, so to speak, her husband's property). This state becomes so painful that, instead of staying home to talk with his wife, the husband hurries out; and as if he had no other place to go, he goes to the tavern to drink blue wine* in the hope of getting drunk, with the other husbands who are just as unhappy as he.[10]

This type of distraction makes things worse. The wife, waiting for payday (Sunday) to buy weekly provisions for the family, is in despair seeing her husband spend most of the money at the tavern. Then she reaches a peak of irritation, and her brutality and wickedness redouble. You have to have personally seen these working-class households (especially the bad ones) to have an idea of the husband's misfortune and the wife's suffering. It passes from reproaches and insults to blows, then tears; from discouragement to despair.[11]

And following the acute chagrins caused by the husband come the pregnancies, illnesses, unemployment, and poverty, planted by the door like Medusa's head. Add to all that the endless tension provoked by four or five loud, turbulent, and bothersome children clamoring about their mother, in a small worker's room too small to turn around in. My! One would have to be an angel from heaven not to be irritated, not to become brutal and mean in such a situation. However, in this domestic setting, what becomes of the children? They see their father only in the evening or on Sunday. Always either upset or drunk, their father speaks to them only angrily and gives them only insults and blows. Hearing their mother continuously complain, they begin to feel hatred and scorn for her. They fear and obey her, but they do not love her, for a person is made that way—he cannot love someone who mistreats him. And isn't it a great misfortune for a child not to be able to love his mother! If he is unhappy, to whose breast will he go to cry? If he thoughtlessly makes a bad mistake

* *Vin bleu*, the rough, cheap wine served in Paris taverns during the nineteenth century.

or is led astray, in whom can he confide? Having no desire to stay close to his mother, the child will seek any pretext to leave the parental home. Bad associations are easy to make, for girls as for boys. Strolling becomes vagrancy, and vagrancy often becomes thievery.

Among the poor girls in houses of prostitution and the poor men moaning in jails, how many can say, "If we had had a *mother able to raise us*, then we would not be here."

I repeat, woman is everything in the life of a worker. As mother, she can influence him during his childhood. She and only she is the one from whom he gets his first notions of that science which is so important to acquire—the science of life, which teaches us how to live well for ourselves and for others, according to the milieu in which fate has placed us.[12] As lover, she can influence him during his youth, and what a powerful influence could be exerted by a young, beautiful, and beloved girl! As wife, she can have an effect on him for three-quarters of his life. Finally, as daughter, she can act upon him in his old age. Note that the worker's position is very different from an idle person's. If the rich child has a mother unable to raise him, he is placed in a boarding school or given a governess. If the young rich fellow has no mistress, he can busy his heart and imagination with studying the arts and sciences. If the rich man has no spouse, he does not fail to find distractions in society. If the old rich man has no daughter, he finds some old friends or young nephews who willingly come and play cards with him; whereas the worker, for whom all these pleasures are denied, has only the company of the women in his family, his companions in misfortune, for all his joy and solace. The result of this situation is that it would be most important, from the point of view of intellectually, morally, and materially improving the working class, that the women receive from childhood a rational and solid education, apt to develop all their potential so that they can become skilled in their trades, good mothers capable of raising and guiding their children

and to be for them, as *La Presse* says, free and natural schoolteach-
ers, and also so that they can serve as moralizing agents for the
men whom they influence from birth to death.

Are you beginning to understand, you men, who cry scandal
before being willing to examine the issue, why I demand rights
for women? Why I would like women placed in society on a
footing of *absolute equality* with men to enjoy the legal birthright
all beings have? I call for woman's rights because I am convinced
that *all* the misfortunes in the world come from this neglect and
scorn shown until now for the natural and inalienable rights of
woman. I call for woman's rights because it is the only way to
have her educated, and woman's education depends upon man's
in general, and particularly the working-class man's. I call for
woman's rights because it is the only way to obtain her rehabilitation before the church, the law, and society, and this rehabilitation is necessary before working men themselves can be
rehabilitated. All working-class ills can be summed up in two
words: poverty and ignorance. Now in order to get out of this
maze, I see only one way: begin by educating women, because
the women are in charge of instructing boys and girls.

Workers, in the current state of things, you know what goes
on in your households. You, the master with rights over your
wife, do you live with her with a contented heart? Say, are you
happy? No, it is easy to see, in spite of your rights, you are
neither contented nor happy. Between master and slave there can
only be the weariness of the chain's weight tying them together.
Where the lack of freedom is felt, happiness cannot exist.

Men always complain about the bad moods and the devious
and silently wicked characters women show in all their relationships. Oh, would I have a very bad opinion of women, if in the
state of abjection where the law and customs place them, they
were to submit without a murmur to the yoke weighing on them!
Thanks be to God, that it is not so! Their protest, since the
beginning of time, has always been relentless. But since the dec-

laration of the rights of man, a solemn act proclaiming the neglect
and scorn the new men gave to women, their protest has taken
on new energy and violence which proves that the slave's exasperation has peaked.[13]

Workers, you who have good sense and with whom one can
reason, because, as Fourier says, you do not have minds stuffed
with systems, suppose for a moment that by right woman is the
equal of man? What would come of that? (1) That as soon as one
would no longer have to fear the dangerous consequences necessarily caused by the moral and physical development of woman's
faculties because of her current enslavement, she would be carefully educated so as to bring out the best possible in her intelligence and work; (2) that you, men of the people, you would have
clever workers for mothers, earning a good wage, instructed,
well-raised and very able to teach and raise you, workers, as it
is appropriate for free men; (3) that your sisters, lovers, wives,
and friends would be educated, well-raised women whose daily
companionship would be most pleasant for you, for nothing is
sweeter or gentler to a man's heart than a woman's conversation
when she is well educated, good, and speaks with logic and
benevolence.

We have quickly glanced over what is currently going on in the
workers' households. Let us now examine what would occur in
these same households if woman were man's equal.

Knowing that his wife has rights equal to his, the husband
would not treat her anymore with the disdain and scorn shown
to inferiors. On the contrary, he would treat her with the respect
and deference one grants to equals. Then the woman will no
longer have cause for irritation; and once that is destroyed, she
will no longer appear brutal, devious, grouchy, angry, exasperated, or mean. No longer considered the husband's servant at
home, but his associate, friend, and companion, she will naturally take an interest in the association and do all she can to make
the little household flourish. With theoretical and practical

knowledge, she will employ all her intelligence to keep her house neat, economical, and pleasant. Educated and aware of the utility of an education, she will put all her ambition into raising her children well. She will lovingly teach them herself, watch over their schoolwork, and place them in good apprenticeships; and finally, she will always guide them with care, tenderness, and discernment. Then what a contented heart, peace of mind, and happy soul the man, the husband, the worker will have who possesses such a woman! Finding his wife has intelligence, common sense and educated opinions, he will be able to talk with her about serious subjects, tell her about his plans, and work with her to further improve their position. Flattered by his confidence in her, she will help him with good advice or collaboration in his endeavors and business. The worker, also educated and well brought up, will find it delightful to teach and develop his young children. Workers in general are kindhearted and love children very much. How diligently a man will work all week knowing that he is to spend Sunday in his wife's company, that he will enjoy his two little mischievous, affectionate girls and his two already educated boys who are able to talk with their father about serious things! How hard this father will work to earn a few extra cents to buy pretty bonnets for his little girls, a book for his sons, an engraving or something else which he knows will please them? With what joyful ecstasy these little gifts will be received, and what happiness for the mother to see the reciprocal love between father and children! It is clear that this, hypothetically, would be the most desirable domestic life for the worker. Comfortable at home, happy and satisfied in the company of his kind, old mother and young wife and children, it would never occur to him to leave the house to seek a good time at the tavern, that place of perdition which wastes the worker's time, money and health, and dulls his intellect. With half of what a drunkard spends in the tavern, a worker's whole family living together could go for meals in the country in summer. So little is necessary for people who know how to live soberly. Out in the open air, the children would all be happy to run with their father and mother, who would be like children to amuse them; and in the evening, with contented hearts and limbs slightly weary from the week's work, the family would return home very satisfied with their day. In winter, the family would go to a show. These amusements offer a dual advantage: they instruct children while entertaining them. How many objects of study an intelligent mother can find to teach her children in a day spent in the country or an evening at the theater!

Under the circumstances I have just outlined, the home would create well-being rather than ruin for the worker. Who doesn't know how love and contentment of the heart treble or quadruple a man's strength? We have seen it in a few rare cases. It has happened that a worker, adoring his family and getting the idea of teaching his children, did the work that three unmarried men would not have been able to do in order to attain this noble goal. Then there is the question of deprivations. Single men spend generously; they don't deny themselves anything. What does it matter, they say, after all, we can gaily live and drink since we have no one to feed. But the married man who loves his family finds satisfaction in depriving himself and lives with exemplary frugality.

Workers, this vaguely sketched picture of the situation the proletariat would enjoy if woman were recognized as man's equal must lead to thought about the evil existing and the goodness which might exist. That ought to make you become very determined.

Workers, you probably have no power to abrogate the old laws or to make new ones. But you have the power to protest against the inequity and absurdity of laws that impede humanity's progress and make you in particular suffer. You can and must then energetically use thought, speaking, and writing to protest the laws oppressing you for it is your sacred duty. So now, try to understand: the law which enslaves woman and deprives her of education oppresses you, proletarian men.

To be raised, educated, and taught the science of the world, the son of the wealthy has governesses and knowledgeable teachers, able advisers and finally, beautiful *marquises*, elegant, witty women whose functions in high society consist in taking over the son's education after he leaves school. It's a very useful role for the well-being of those gentlemen of high nobility. These ladies teach them to have proper manners, tact, finesse, wit; in a word, they make them into men who *know how to live*, the right kind of men. No matter how capable a young man is, if he is fortunate enough to be the protégé of one of these amiable ladies, his fortune is made. At thirty-five he is certain of becoming an ambassador or a minister. While you, poor workers, to rear and teach you, you have only your mother; to make you into civilized men, you only have women of your class, your companions in ignorance and misery.[14]

Thus it is not in the name of woman's superiority (as I will unfailingly be accused) that I tell you to demand rights for women; not really. First of all, before discussing her superiority, one must recognize her social individuality. My support has a more solid basis. In the name of your own interest and improvement, men; and finally in the name of the universal well-being of all men and women, I invite you to appeal for women's rights, and meanwhile at least to recognize them in principle.

Thus, workers, it is up to you, who are the victims of real inequality and injustice, to establish the rule of justice and absolute equality between man and woman on this earth. Give a great example to the world, an example that will prove to your oppressors that you want to triumph through your right and not by brute force. You seven, ten, fifteen million proletarians, could avail yourselves of that brute force! In calling for justice, prove that you are just and equitable. You, the strong men, the men with bare arms, proclaim your recognition that woman is your equal, and as such, you recognize her equal right to the benefits of the *universal union of working men and women.*

Workers, perhaps in three or four years you will have your first palace, ready to admit six hundred old persons and six hundred children. Well! Proclaim through your statutes, which will become your charter, the rights of women for equality. Let it be written in your charter that an equal number of girls and boys will be admitted to the Workers' Union palace to receive intellectual and vocational training.

Workers, in 1791, your fathers proclaimed the immortal declaration of the *rights of man,* and it is to that solemn declaration that today you owe your being free and equal men before the law. May your fathers be honored for this great work! But, proletarians, there remains for you men of 1843 a no less great work to finish. In your turn, emancipate the last slaves still remaining in French society; proclaim the *rights of woman,* in the same terms your fathers proclaimed yours:

"We, French proletarians, after fifty-three years of experience, recognize that we are duly enlightened and convinced that the neglect and scorn perpetrated upon the natural rights of woman are the only cause of unhappiness in the world, and we have resolved to expose her sacred and inalienable rights in a solemn declaration inscribed in our charter. We wish women to be informed of our declaration, so that they will not let themselves be oppressed and degraded any more by man's injustice and tyranny, and so that men will respect the freedom and equality they enjoy in their wives and mothers.

1. The goal of society necessarily being the common happiness of men and women, the Workers' Union guarantees them the enjoyment of their rights as working men and women.

2. Their rights include equal admission to the Workers' Union palaces, whether they be children, or disabled or elderly.

3. Woman being man's equal, we understand that girls will

receive as rational, solid, and extensive (though different) an education in moral and professional matters as the boys.

4. As for the disabled and the elderly, in every way, the treatment will be the same for women as for men.*

Workers, rest assured, if you have enough equity and justice
to inscribe in your Charter the few lines I have just traced, this
declaration of the rights of woman will soon become custom, then
law, and within twenty-five years you will see absolute equality
of man and woman inscribed at the head of the book of law.

Then, my brothers, and only then, will human unity be
established.

Sons of '89, that is the work your fathers bequeathed to you!

NOTES

1. Aristotle, less tender than Plato, asked this question without
answering it: Do women have souls? The Council of Mâcon deigned
to decide in their favor by a margin of three votes (*La Phalange*,
August 21, 1842).

Thus, with three fewer votes, woman would have been seen as
belonging to the realm of beasts, and this being so, man, the lord
and master, would have been obliged to cohabit with the beast!
That thought makes one shudder and freeze in horror! Besides,
given the way things are, that ought to be a subject of deep grief,
for the wise among the wise to think that they descend from the
female race. For, if they are really convinced that woman is as
stupid as they claim, what a shame for them to have been conceived within such a creature, to have suckled her milk and remained under her tutelage for a good part of their lives! So! It is
very likely that if those sages had been able to place woman
outside nature as they placed her outside the Church, the law,

* Tristan probably was not familiar with a 24-page feminist declaration, *Les Droits de la femme*, written by Olympe de Gouges in 1788
and addressed to the Queen. She did know, however, Mary Woll-
stonecraft's work, which she greatly admired and whose neglect she
lamented (cf. *Promenades dans Londres*, the chapter on English women).

and society, they would have been spared the shame of descending from her. But unfortunately there is the law of God above the wisdom of the sages.

Except for Jesus, all the prophets treated woman with inexplicable iniquity, scorn, and harshness. Moses has his God say, "I will greatly multiply your pain in childbearing; in pain you shall bring forth children, yet your desire shall be for your husband, and he shall rule over you" (*Genesis*, III, 16).

The author of *Ecclesiastes* had pushed the pride of his sex so far as to say, "Better a vicious man than a virtuous woman."

In the name of his God, Mohammed says: "Men are superior to women because of the qualities by which God has raised the former over the latter, and because men use their riches to pamper women.

You will reprimand the women whose disobedience you fear; you will relegate them to separate beds, you will beat them; but as soon as they obey, do not try to quarrel with them" (*Koran*, IV, 38).

Manu's laws say, "During childhood, a woman must depend upon her father; in her youth she depends upon her husband; her husband deceased, on her sons; if she has no son, the closest relatives of her husband, or lacking them, those of her father. If she has no paternal relatives, then the ruler: a woman must never govern herself by herself!" Here is the most curious thing: "She must always be good-humored." [According to Hindu theosophy, Manu is a great Being (though once a man) who governs the Earth. He is the reputed author of the famed Hindu law book, which is essentially a system of cosmogony and includes among its twelve books sections on marriage and wifely duties.—*Trans.*]

> *215.* A woman cannot go to court without her husband's permission, even if she has her own business or maintains herself.

> *37.* Official witnesses for birth, marriage, and death certificates can only be of the male sex (*Code civil*).

One (man) must be active and strong, the other (woman) *passive* and weak (J.-J. Rousseau, *Emile*).

This formula is reproduced in the Code:

213. The husband owes protection to his wife, the wife obedience to her husband.

2. Most scholars, be they scientists, doctors, or philosophers, have more or less explicitly concluded that women are intellectually inferior.

3. Woman was made for man (Saint Paul).

4. Convinced that neglect and scorn of man's natural rights are the only causes of the world's misfortunes, the French have resolved to proclaim man's sacred and inalienable rights in a declaration. Therefore, each citizen, in a position to compare government's activity with the goal of each social institution, will never submit to oppression or degradation by tyranny. The people will then have a constant and clear view of the foundations underlying their freedom and happiness, of their duties ruled by the magistrates and their mission led by the legislators.

Consequently, they proclaim the following declaration of the rights of man and the citizen in the presence of the Supreme Being:

1. The goal of society is the common good. The Government guarantees man's enjoyment of his natural and unalienable rights.

2. These rights are equality, liberty, security, and property.

3. All men are equal in nature and before the law.

4. The law is the free and solemn expression of the collective will.

5. All the famous generals of the Empire came from the working class. Before 1789, only noblemen were officers.

6. Here is what Fourier said, among other things:

"In the course of my research on society, I found greater reason among women than among men; for women have on several occasions given me new ideas which have afforded me very unexpected solutions to problems.

"Several times I have been indebted to women of the class called quick-witted (the mind which promptly grasps and immediately presents ideas with precision) for precious solutions which had tormented my mind. Men have never been of this kind of help to me.

"Why don't men have that aptitude for new ideas free from prejudice? It is because their minds are enslaved and imprisoned by the biased kind of philosophy learned in school. They leave school with their heads stuffed with principles contradicting nature and cannot independently envision a new idea. If one disagrees with Plato or Seneca, denunciation and excommunication follow for daring to contradict the divine Plato, the divine Cato, or the divine Rato" (*La Fausse Industrie*, p. 326). ["Rato" (*raton* in the original, along with *Platon* and *Caton*) means "little rat."— *Trans.*]

7. From someone licensed to operate an infant school, I learned that according to orders received from on high, the teachers in these sorts of schools are supposed to be more concerned with developing the boys' intellect than with the girls'. Usually all the village schoolmasters treat all the pupils the same. Several have admitted to me that they did receive that order. This is yet another logical consequence of the unequal position occupied by men and women in society. There is a common saying about this: "Well, *for a woman*, she knows quite enough!"

8. Lower-class women prove to be very loving mothers toward their small children until the children reach the age of two or three. Their female instinct makes them understand that during these first two years, the children need continual care. But beyond that age, they brutalize them (except in some cases).

9. It is notable that in all the trades exercised by men and women, the female worker is paid *half* the daily wage of the male worker, or if she does piecework, her wage is half as much. Unable to imagine such a flagrant injustice, we first think this: Because of his muscular strength, the man probably accomplishes twice as much as a woman. Well, reader, it turns out to be exactly the opposite. In all the trades where skill and dexterity are required, women do almost twice as much work as the men. For instance, in printing, *in typesetting* (indeed, they make many mistakes, but that is due to their lack of education), in cotton-spinning to *tie the threads;* in a word, in all the trades which call for a certain lightness of touch, the women excel. One day a printer was tell-

ing me with his quite characteristic naïveté, "They are paid half as much, which is fair because they go *faster* than men; they would earn too much if they were paid the same." Yes, they are paid not for the work they do, but for creating few expenses, for assuming all kinds of deprivations. Workers, you have not seen the disastrous consequences that would result for you from such an injustice done to the detriment of your mothers, sisters, wives, and daughters. What has happened? The factory heads, seeing women working faster and for half pay, dismiss male workers every day from their workshops and replace them with women. And the men cross their arms and die from starvation in the streets. This is how the factory heads proceeded in England. Once on this path, women are let go to be replaced by twelve-year-old children. Half-pay economy! Finally, seven- or eight-year-old children are the only ones being hired. Let one injustice go unheeded, and you can be sure that it will foster thousands more.

10. Why do workers go to taverns? The ruling upper classes have been struck with complete blindness. They refuse to comprehend that their wealth, happiness, and security depend upon the moral, intellectual, and physical improvement of the working class. They dismiss the worker to his misery and ignorance; thinking, according to an old saying, that the cruder the people, the easier to muzzle them. This was all right before the Declaration of the Rights of Man. Since then, it means committing a gross anachronism, a serious mistake. Besides, one ought to be at least logical: if it is believed that it is good and knowledgeable politics to leave the poor class in its raw state, then why recriminate endlessly against its vices? The wealthy accuse the workers of being lazy, debauched, and drunk; and to substantiate their accusations, they exclaim, "If the workers are miserable, it's their own fault. Go to the bars and taverns and you will find them filled with workers drinking and wasting their time." I think that, instead of going to the tavern, if the workers met seven in a room (the number permitted by the September laws), to talk about their common rights and find ways of making them legally valid, the rich would be even more disturbed than by seeing the taverns full.

In the current state of affairs, the tavern is the worker's TEMPLE; it is the only place he can go. He does not believe in the Church; he does not understand anything about the theater. That is why the taverns are always full. In Paris, three-quarters of the workers do not even have a home; they sleep in furnished barracks; and the married ones reside in attics where there is no room or air. Consequently, they are forced to go out, if they want to get a little exercise and fresh air. You do not want to teach the people, you forbid them to meet, in the fear that they will teach themselves or will talk of politics or social doctrines. You do not want them to read, write, or fill their minds with thoughts, for fear that they will revolt! . . . So what do you expect them to do? If you prohibit everything that is mental, it is clear that, as a last resort, there remains only the tavern. Poor workers sometimes go crazy, overwhelmed with misery and sorrows of all kinds at home or with their bosses, or finally because the repugnant and forced work to which they are condemned irritates the nervous system so much. In this state, their only refuge is the tavern, in order to escape from their suffering. So they go to drink blue wine, an execrable medicine whose virtue is the power of *intoxication.*

Before such facts, there are people in the world called virtuous and religious who, comfortably settled in their homes, drink lots of good Bordeaux wine, vintage Chablis, and excellent champagne, at every meal, and those people make a beautiful moral fuss over drunkenness, debauchery, and intemperance in the working class! . . .

In the course of studying the workers (I have been doing this for ten years), never have I encountered a drunkard or real débauché among happily married workers enjoying a certain ease. Whereas, among those who are unhappily married and deeply impoverished, I have found some incorrigible drunkards.

The tavern, therefore, is not the cause of evil, but simply the effect. The cause of evil lies solely in ignorance, misery, and the brutalization of the working class. Instruct the people, and in twenty years the retailers of blue wine will close shop for lack of customers.

In England where the working class is much more ignorant and miserable than in France, the working men and *women* carry the vice of drink as far as dementia; see Eugène Buret on this topic. [Eugène Buret (1811–42), an economist, submitted his two-volume work, *De la Misère des classes laborieuses en France et en Angleterre* (1841) to the "Académie des sciences morales" and won its 1840 contest. It figures prominently on Tristan's recommended reading list, p. 132.—*Trans.*]

11. In support of what I am maintaining here touching on women's brutality and the excellence of their nature, I shall cite an incident which occurred in Bordeaux in 1827 during my stay there.

Among the vegetable vendors holding shop in the open market, there was one woman feared by all the good ones, for she was so insolent, mean, and brutal. Her husband was a garbage collector (which meant that he was a street cleaner and sewage gatherer). One evening he came home and supper was not ready. An argument ensued between the husband and wife. The husband wanted to get to the point with insults, and he struck his wife. At that moment she was cutting up morsels for the soup with a big kitchen knife, and she turned on her husband, piercing his heart. He collapsed, dead. She was taken to prison.

Seeing her husband dead, this very brutal and wicked woman was gripped by such grief and remorse that, despite her crime, she inspired not only compassion but respect in everyone. It was simple to establish that her husband had provoked her, that the murder had been committed in a moment of anger, and not by premeditation. Her grief was such that one feared for her life; and since she was breast-feeding an infant of four months, the judge told her, in order to calm her, that she need not worry, she would be acquitted. But how surprised everyone was when, upon hearing those words, the woman exclaimed, "Me, acquitted! Ah! Your honor, what do you dare say? . . . If an awful woman like me were acquitted, there would be no justice on earth."

One tried everything to reason with her to make her understand that she was not a criminal, since she had not the thought of committing the murder. "Well! What does the thought matter?" she repeated, "if there is a brutalness in me which can make me cripple one of my children or kill my husband? Am I not a dangerous person, incapable of living in society?" Finally, when she was quite convinced that she would be acquitted, this uneducated woman made a resolution worthy of the strongest men in the Roman Republic. She declared that she would take justice into her own hands and *let herself starve to death*. And with what strength and dignity she executed that terrible death sentence she imposed upon herself! Her mother, her family, and her seven children came and tearfully begged her to agree to live for them. She gave her small infant to her mother and said, "Teach my children to be glad to lose such a mother, for, in a moment of brutality, I could kill them as I killed their father." The judges, the priests, the market women, and many others from the town went to her and tried to solicit in her favor. She could not be moved. Then, another means was tried: cakes, fruit, dairy products, wine, and meats were brought to her room. Even some chicken was roasted and brought piping hot so the aroma would entice her to eat. "Everything you're doing is useless," she repeated with great coolness and dignity. "A woman who is brutal enough to kill the father of her seven children must die, and I will die." She suffered awful torment without complaining, and on the seventh day, she expired.

12. Here is how *La Phalange* spoke about a very remarkable article in *La Presse*, on September 11, 1842:

"*La Presse* made the wise decision to table the futile quarrels over the small session, on the type of voting on the investigation and the regency law, or on Monsieur Thiers's conversion, and has begun to study the questions that are going to be submitted to the general councils. . . . Today, many children are still deprived of education, and 4,196 townships have no school. To take any excuses away from the parents and in order to win over the lack of caring and bad will of some municipal councils, the *Presse* editor proposes that the monthly fee paid by the pupils be eliminated, and he calls for the establishment and maintenance of all schools to cease being the concern of the townships and be henceforth part of the State budget. We have always stated that society owes an education to all its members, and it is quite deplorable that the government of an enlightened country itself cannot see that, without fail, children be given the necessary care for their development. We quote the end of the *Presse* article; this journal's reflections on education for women are correct and do it honor. On every occasion we have always protested that odious and stupid abandonment of a *whole sex*, of which our so-called civilized and in many respects truly barbarous society has been guilty.

" 'Besides this important reform, there is another, perhaps more urgent, that the general councils also ought to recommend to the administration and the chambers; we wish to speak of the organization of primary schools for girls. Is it not strange that a country like France, which sees itself in the vanguard of civilization, which seeks to prove it by spreading the light of instruction for all classes of citizens, which opens schools everywhere for children and their teachers, also completely neglects to educate the women, the earliest teachers of children? This neglect is not only an injustice, it is an imprudence, an error. In fact, what is the result of the ignorance of most mothers? That when their sons are five years old and start school, they come with a bunch of bad habits, absurd beliefs, and false ideas sucked with their mother's milk. And the schoolmaster has more trouble getting rid of these than he has teaching them to read. So in the long run, *it costs more money and time to get rid of an injustice* and have *bad pupils* than to *instruct women*, while making them *more adept workers, more efficient housekeepers, and the natural, free teachers of school lessons.' "

13. Read the *Gazette des Tribunaux*. That is where, before the facts, one must study the state of exasperation manifested today by women. [In the issue of February 1, 1839, Tristan's personal story of domestic oppression appeared, as revealed during her husband's trial for attempted murder.—*Trans.*]

14. I have just shown that woman's ignorance has the most dangerous consequences. I maintain that the emancipation of the workers is impossible as long as women remain in this state of abjection. They inhibit all progress. Sometimes I have witnessed violent scenes between husband and wife. I have often been the victim of it, receiving the most crude insults. Those poor creatures, not seeing beyond the tips of their noses, as it is said, got

angry with their husbands, and with me, because the worker wasted a few hours of his time being concerned with political or social ideas. "Why do you need to get involved in things that don't concern you?" they exclaim. "Think about earning enough to eat and let the world be."

This is cruel to say, but I know some unhappy workers, men with hearts, intelligence, and good will, who would like nothing better than to devote their Sundays and small savings to serving the cause, and who, in order to have peace at home, hide from their wives and mothers the fact that they come to see me and write to me. These same women detest me, say awful things about me, and if they did not fear prison, maybe their zeal would push them to coming and insulting and beating me; and all that, because I commit the big crime, they say, of putting ideas in their men's heads which move them to read, write and speak among themselves, all useless things that are a waste of time. It's deplorable! However, I have met a few women who are capable of understanding the social issues and who show themselves to be dedicated. [One of the abusive wives in question, Madame Gosset, is mentioned by Puech: Tristan "had to undergo a violent scene from Mme. Gosset, upset for a month because her husband was wasting his time over an idea; also perhaps because the idea belonged to a young, seductive woman . . ." (p. 148).—*Trans.*]

IV

Plan for the Universal Unionization of Working Men and Women

I am going to provide a quick glimpse of the steps to be followed if one wishes promptly to consolidate the Workers' Union on a solid footing.

Let it be understood that I am not claiming to trace a definitive, unalterable plan. A plan totally spelled out in advance can never be realized. Only in the process can one appreciate the most appropriate means to achieve the enterprise's success. To shape, cut back and affirm in theory only imply to me extreme unawareness of the difficulties of implementation.

However, as it is natural for the person who conceived of an idea to grasp its entire scope and understand all its ramifications, I believe I must pose some guidelines to alleviate many difficulties and to help set up the Workers' Union.

In order to locate more readily the paragraphs that might have to be consulted, I have decided to number them. This format will appear perhaps a bit strange for I do not mean to list statutes here: just as for the rest of the work, I hereby entreat the reader not to forget that I had to, and in fact did, focus on the *content*. I felt that in order to treat such issues well, I had to limit myself to being clear and concise, and shy away from certain stylistic effects; formal elegance would have detracted from my subject.

Wanting to *convince*, I had to use logic; and logic is the sworn enemy of so-called *poetic form*. This is why I carefully avoided using a pleasing form which, in the long run, does not prove anything, and leaves the reader enchanted but not convinced.

To make my idea clearer, I am dividing the plan's outline into parts, with a summary at the beginning so the principal points can be grasped at a glance.

SUMMARY

A. How the Workers Must Proceed to Establish the Workers' Union
B. How the Workers' Union Must Proceed from the Financial Point of View
C. The Intellectual Point of View
D. On the Use of Funds
E. Building the Palaces
F. Conditions for Admission to the Palaces for the Elderly, the Disabled, and Children
G. Labor Organization in the Palaces
H. Moral, Intellectual, and Vocational Instruction to Be Given to the Children
I. The Inevitable Results of This Education

A. *How the Workers Must Proceed to Establish the Workers' Union*

1. In their respective trade, union, or welfare groups,[1] the workers must begin by forming one or several committees (according to the number of members) composed of seven members (five men and two women),[2] chosen from the most capable.

2. These committees may not receive any contributions. Their function will be temporarily limited to inscribing in a great reg-

ister book the sex, age, names, addresses, and occupations of all those who want to become members of the Workers' Union, and the amount each pledges to contribute.

3. That the person in question is a working man or woman must be verified in order to have a name put in the book.[3] And by working man or woman, we mean any individual who *works with his or her hands* in any fashion. Thus, servants, porters, messengers, laborers, and all the so-called odd-jobbers will be considered workers. Only soldiers and sailors will have to be exempted. Here are the reasons for this exception: (*a*) the State comes to the aid of soldiers and sailors through the disabled fund; (*b*) and the soldiers are knowledgeable only in destructive work and the sailors in sea work, so neither would be usefully employed in the Workers' Union palace.

4. Yet, since the soldiers and sailors belong to the working class and by this reason have the right to adhere to the Workers' Union, they will be inscribed separately as brothers. They may contribute toward their children's admission to the palaces. In a third book, all those who want to cooperate in the prosperity of the working class will be entered as sympathizers.

5. In no case may the professional beggar put his name on the list. But the workers who have signed up at the welfare office and who receive aid because their work is not enough to support their families may not be excluded. Misfortune is respectable; only idleness debases and degrades and must be pitilessly rejected.

6. In view of the Union, and this is of the utmost importance, the workers must make it their duty and mission to use all their influence to get their mothers, wives, sisters, daughters, and girl friends to join in with them. They themselves must urge them and escort them to the committee so that they can enter their names in the Union's great-book. That is a proper mission for the workers.

7. As soon as the working men and women are represented by the committees they will have elected, these committees will then

elect a central committee from among themselves for all of France. Its headquarters will be in Paris or Lyons (in the city with the most workers). This committee will be composed of fifty members (forty men and ten women) nominated from the most capable.

8. It is agreed that not all of the working class must be represented by committees in order to nominate the central committee. Thus for Paris, it suffices for an adequate number of working men and women to be represented in order to proceed to electing the central committee.[4]

9. Once the central committee is elected, the Workers' Union will be established.

B. How the Workers' Union Must Proceed from the Financial Point of View

10. The central committee's first act must be to give the order to all the branch committees to turn over the great register books listing the names and pledges to designated attorneys or bankers (by district), so that every Workers' Union member can contribute his amount into safe hands on Sundays or Monday mornings.[5]

11. For the accounting that will be necessitated by the endless contributions, the savings bank system will be adopted insofar as it is possible.

12. Men will be appointed and paid to collect the contributions in the workplaces and homes, and they will have to be bonded.

13. The central committee's second act must be to seek four persons in or outside the Union, men or women, with the following: (a) good will and dedication, (b) intelligence and ability, (c) true knowledge of the working-class mind and situation, (d) activity and eloquence of a kind to influence the workers. The central committee will vest in these four its full powers and send them throughout France. They will be called the Workers' Union envoys. Their mission will be to create committees organized ex-

actly on the same basis as those in Paris in all the towns, villages, boroughs, and hamlets.

14. For this mission, the central committee will allocate an annual salary to the envoys or enough to cover their travel.

15. In order to simplify administrative activity as much as possible and also to make surveillance easier and more active, the committees in the small towns, villages, and hamlets will correspond with the head-towns[6] in their departments, and the committees in these head-towns will report to the central committee on the operations of the small committees.

16. As to how to gather the contributions and forward them to the central committee, nothing is easier. Upon receiving the funds, the attorneys will deposit them with the tax collectors in the towns and the latter will pass them on to the central committee. In this way, considerable amounts can be sent from one end of France to the other at very little cost.[7]

17. As for investing these funds, I shall abstain from saying anything right now. I admit that I am too realistic to calculate something that does not yet exist. The central committee will temporarily be required to place the funds it receives in Government bonds so that it does not lose interest on the money.

18. Three general inspectors will be appointed to oversee the financial operation of the central committee; and, at the end of each year, they will publish a report to be distributed to all the Union committees.

19. These few lines are enough, I think, to give an idea of the financial organization that I have conceived for the Workers' Union. Now, let us move on to intellectual matters.

C. The Intellectual Point of View

20. In the second chapter I stated that the Workers' Union was to begin by gaining representation before the country. Now, as soon as it is financially established, it must proceed to the ap-

pointment of its defender. "But," I shall be asked, "how can you name a defender if there is no money to pay him?" Well! In that case, I think the central committee can easily request six months or a year of credit from its defender. The central committee must not be obstructed by a lack of funds. What man would dare refuse credit to a Workers' Union that had chosen him to defend the sacred cause? *Not one*, rest assured. Then the defender will be well aware that his very appointment will bring two, three, or four million workers to the Workers' Union who otherwise might not join. Yes, because do not forget that the defender, appointed and paid by the Union, will be living proof that the working class is truly unified. As of then, its strength and power can no longer be questioned; and once they are recognized, the incredulous and unconcerned workers (and this is the majority) will have no more doubts. Full of hope, they will come with their contributions. It is the story of the successful venture: everyone wants stock in it. It is the story of Panurge's sheep: if the shepherd can get a dozen to go in, the rest follow by themselves.* So the defender must be appointed immediately, and, I repeat, if there is any reluctance or backing off, the Union will be set back fifty years.

21. As soon as the defender is appointed, the central committee must appeal to the King of France, as head of State; to the members of the Catholic clergy, as the leaders of a religion based on a truly democratic principle; to the nobility, as the most generous and charitable in the nation; to the manufacturers, as indebted to the workers for their fortunes; to the financiers, as indebted to the workers for their wealth, as the workers' labor has made the financiers' money worth something; to the landowners, as indebted to the workers whose labor has made their land valuable;

* In Rabelais's *Pantagruel*, Panurge (legendary for his bawdiness) takes revenge on Dindenault, a sheep merchant who had insulted him, by buying his best sheep, throwing it into the sea, and watching the rest of Dindenault's sheep follow to their death.

and finally to the bourgeois, too, who live off and get rich by the labor of the workers.

22. These appeals will have a dual purpose: first, to obtain contributions to the Workers' Union fund through donations as an expression of the so-called upper classes' gratitude to the working class. This money would speed up the building of the Workers' Union palaces. Second, these donations and the refusal to donate would show which classes are sympathetic to the Workers' Union or disapproving. At this time, it is very important for the working class to know exactly what to expect with regard to the sympathy or animosity the other social classes might have toward it.

23. Here is the outline for these sorts of appeals as I conceive of them. It is up to the central committee to modify them, as they see fit.

24. APPEAL TO THE KING OF FRANCE, as the appointed national ruler[8]

Sire,

In accepting the title of King, the ancient kings of France contracted the sacred duty, as military leaders, of bravely defending the nation against enemy attack. During times of war France belonged in fact to two privileged classes, the nobility and the clergy. Lords, barons, noblemen, and bishops were the religious, military, and civic leaders, and they alone governed the commoners as they saw fit and as they pleased. Serfs, peasants, villagers and even the bourgeois were subjected to their domination. Of course, the despotism of the lords weighed heavily in grief and suffering over the commoners . . . However, while receiving whippings from his master, the serf also got bread to eat, clothes to wear, wood for heating, and a roof over his head.

Sire, today things are different. There is no King of France anymore, no more barons, no more bishops. The people are no longer whipped; they are free and are all equal before the law.

Yes—but without the right to work, they are exposed to dying of hunger!

In 1830, the nation's representatives, considering it a time of peace, liberty, equality and work, and no longer seeing a need for a military leader, pronounced the fall of the King of France. And in the midst of the Chamber of Deputies they elected a king for the French.[9]

Sire, in accepting the title of King of the French, you contracted the sacred obligation of defending the interests of all the French. Sire, in the name of the mandate you received from the French people, the Workers' Union has come to call your Majesty's attention to the fact that the sufferings of the most populous and useful class have been hidden from you. The Workers' Union asks for no privilege; it simply requests the recognition of a right it has been denied and without which its life is in jeopardy; it asks for the RIGHT TO WORK.

Sire, as head of State, you can propose a bill. You can ask the Chambers to pass a law granting the RIGHT TO WORK for all men and women.

Sire, by recognizing that the interests of the most populous class must, in the general interest, prevail over all partisan interests, hitherto the only to be heard, you will establish a duty from which none of your successors will attempt to deviate. You will thus insure the strongest support for the July Monarchy, the greatest degree of power and wealth to France, the highest morality for the nation. For the crown's stability, France's power and wealth, the moral beauty of the national character, and the prosperity of the whole nation depend upon the extent of vocational and ethical training given to the most populous and useful class.

As head of State, you can provide a shining sign of sympathy and gratitude to the Workers' Union. Sire, you own several magnificent estates located on French soil; you could immortalize your name by offering one of your beautiful properties to the

Workers' Union as a mark of your sympathy and gratitude to the most populous and useful class so it can build its first palace. A queen of England gave one of her palaces to the old sailors who had made the wealth and glory of the British Empire so that they would have a place to die in peace.[10] Louis the Great built the Hôtel des Invalides; it is now up to the Citizen King to raise the first Workers' Union palace.

Sire, by acting thus, you will provide a grand and healthy example which all future heads of State will be *forced to imitate*. This act of generosity will proclaim that the kings' primary duty is to be concerned with the defense of the interests of the most populous and useful class.

25. To the Catholic clergy

Catholic priests,

The Workers' Union has come to request your aid and support.

Weary of fighting and violent reactions, the French proletarians today are seeking in the union's fraternity a remedy for their misery. Catholic priests, in this great work, be Christ's apostles for them. Help with your influence and power; the working class appeals to you, and, in turn, it will help you reconstruct your Church on solid ground. Catholic priests, you are vital insofar as you act in accordance with the principle you represent: democracy. Preaching for the people, you will be powerful and revered; whereas, preaching for the rich, you will be weak and distrusted. So declare yourselves the defenders of the most populous and useful class. That is your duty, your holy mission: Catholic priests, prove yourselves worthy of it.

In the name of Christ, your master; in the name of the apostles who established the Church by risking their lives preaching equality, brotherhood, and UNITY; in the name of the Church Fathers who, listening only to their duty, forbade the entrance to the temple to emperors stained by the blood of their people; in the name of the great medieval pontiffs who banned tyrannical kings; in the name of the famous orators, your oracles, Bossuet,

Massillon, Bourdaloue, Father Bridaine,* who frightened the aristocracy by speaking to them of God's awful judgments on pride, and humbled the princes' pomp by severely reminding them that the Christian's first duty is charity for the poor; in the name of all this Catholic history, the Workers' Union asks you to become again *Christian priests* for it.

We know that the term *Catholic Church* means *universal association;* that the word *communion* means *universal brotherhood;* we know that the Catholic Church is based on the principle of UNITY and has as its goal the fusion of all peoples so as to consolidate the world through a great religious, social body. Catholic priests, it is up to you to realize the great notions of UNITY posed by Christ and his apostles. Think about it; you cannot do this work unless you become priests to the most populous and useful class. The Workers' Union is pursuing absolutely the same goal as the Catholic Church. The Workers' Union wants peace, brotherhood, and equality among all—HUMAN UNITY. Catholic priests, if you are truly men of peace and real Catholics, your place is among the people. You must march with them and at their head.

You priests, who have huge churches where the townspeople and peasants gather, you who can speak from your pulpits to both the rich and poor, preach justice to the rich and unity to the poor.

However, understand that the proletarians do not ask the ten million owners for alms. No, they are calling for the right to work; so once assured of always being able to make a living, they will no longer be debased and degraded by the alms the wealthy scornfully throw to them.

Catholic priests, if you will, you can hasten the construction of

* Jacques Bénigne Bossuet (1627–1704) served as the royal prince's tutor and became Bishop of Meaux; Jean-Baptiste Massillon (1663–1742) was a preacher known for the strictness of his ideas; Louis Bourdaloue (1632–1704), a Jesuit priest, wrote *Sermons;* and Father Jacques Bridaine (1701–67) was a preacher acclaimed for his powerful eloquence.

the first Workers' Union palace. To do that, you have only to preach unity in humanity, brotherhood in humanity, and equality for all. What a beautiful mission! Then you will have the right to enjoy the people's love, their recognition, offerings and blessings; for then, you will truly be the priests of the people.

26. To the French nobility

French nobility,

We poor proletarians, who have been your servants from one generation to the next, know by experience that for you generosity of the heart is a question of blood, just like courage and elegant manners. This is why the Workers' Union has confidently come to request your cooperation in building its first palace. You noble lords, who live in vast, magnificent townhouses and own castles throughout France worthy of being royal residences, you who live in princely luxury, would you refuse to give some small part of your excess to the laborers who work your lands, weave your rich velvets and silks, cultivate your magnificent greenhouses so you can have beautiful fruit and flowers in every season, take care of your forests, horses, and dogs so you can take pleasure in hunting—in a word, work fourteen hours a day so that you can inexpensively enjoy all the superfluousness of the most refined luxury?

No, you probably will not refuse us. One of your great merits is knowing how to give. The Workers' Union will gratefully receive the gracious offerings you willingly send for its first palace.

27. To the manufacturers

Sirs and Employers,

By making us work, you and your families live like English bankers. You amass more or less huge fortunes. In working for you, we can scarcely survive and feed our poor families. This is a legal issue. Thus, take note that we are not blaming or accusing you; we are simply observing what is. Today at last the workers are aware of the cause of their pains, and in their wish to put a stop to them, they have UNITED.

The Workers' Union has judged that it has to make an appeal to the generosity of the employers. It thought that the gentlemen owning the factories, deeply conscious of the gratitude they owe the working class, would be pleased to show a mark of their sympathy. The Workers' Union, motivated by purely fraternal feelings and completely peaceful intentions, has reason to be able to count on your support. Thus it confidently has come to ask you for your real patronage and active cooperation. If the proprietors would like to offer the Workers' Union gifts, either money or in kind, their gifts, whatever they may be, would be gratefully received.

28. To the Financiers, owners, and bourgeois

This would be the same letter as above in substance with a few variations in the form.

29. Finally, the central committee ought to make a last appeal, the one I would count on the most,[11] to women.

30. Appeal to women of all stations, ages, opinions, and countries

Women,

You, whose souls, hearts, minds, and senses are so impressionable that, without realizing it, you shed a tear for all suffering, a cry for all moaning, sublime enthusiasm for all generous acts, devotion for all ills, a consoling word for all the afflicted, you women who are devoured by the need to love, act, and live, you who seek everywhere an outlet for that burning, endless activity which inspires, yet consumes and destroys you, women, will you remain silent and always hidden, when the most populous and useful class, your proletarian brothers and sisters, working, suffering, weeping, and moaning, come and beg you to help them leave their misery and ignorance?

Women, the Workers' Union has looked your way. It has understood that it cannot have more devoted, intelligent, and powerful allies. Women, the Workers' Union has a right to your gratitude. It was the first to recognize *in theory* women's rights. Today its cause and yours are becoming one and the same. Rich women, educated, intelligent, enjoying the power afforded by instruction, merit, status, and wealth, who can influence your men, children, servants, and workers, lend your powerful protection to the men who have only numbers and rights to make them strong. In turn, these men with bare arms will lend you their support. You are oppressed by law and prejudice. Unite with the oppressed, and this legitimate, sacred alliance will enable us to struggle legally and loyally against oppressive laws and prejudices.

Women, what is your mission in society? None. Well, do you want a worthy way to spend your life? Devote it to the victory of the most sacred of causes: the Workers' Union.

Women, who feel that holy fire called faith, love, devotion, intelligence, and action, you must become the preachers for the Workers' Union.

Women writers, poets, artists, write to instruct the people and use the union as the text for your songs.

Rich women, get rid of all those cosmetic frivolities absorbing enormous sums and learn to use your wealth more effectively and magnificently. Donate to the Workers' Union.

Women of the people, join the Workers' Union. Enlist your daughters and sons to sign up in the union book.

Women of all of France and the whole earth, place your glory in proudly and publicly becoming the defenders of the union.

Oh, women, our sisters, do not remain deaf of our appeal! Come to us, we need your help, assistance, and protection.

Women, in the name of your suffering and ours, we ask for your cooperation in our great work.

31. The central committee might also make an appeal to artists. They are usually very generous. They could give their cooperation in constructing the first palace and decorating it with their paintings and sculpture. The dramatic artists and musicians could

give shows and concerts to benefit the Workers' Union, and the proceeds would be used to buy blocks of marble, canvases, paint, and everything necessary for the artists to carry out their work.

32. The central committee will have to add the necessary legal and solemn tone to these appeals. First they must bear the signatures of all the committees in France. Then the central committee will go on foot and in full regalia[12] to see the King. A man and a woman holding hands as a sign of union will present the appeal to the King. Then, a man and a woman carrying a big book (the book of pledges) will present it to the King so he can write his name and his contributions to the Workers' Union. Then the president of the Workers' Union will beseech the King to introduce the representatives from the Workers' Union to the Queen and the ladies of the royal family so that they can inscribe their names and gifts below the King's.

33. After leaving the King, the central committee will hold a meeting to edit the proceedings of what was said and done during the visit to the palace. The fifty committee members will sign it, and then 500,000 copies of the appeal will be published along with the proceedings. The central committee will send a certain number of copies to each committee in France to be distributed evenly and free of charge throughout France.

34. The same procedure should be followed for all the other appeals. The committee will go to the Archbishop of Paris to present similarly the gift book; then to the chief members of the French nobility residing in Paris; as well as to artists, manufacturers, bankers, landowners, and the bourgeois represented by their respective bodies, Chambers of Commerce, attorneys, lawyers, etc. As for the women: since in the present society they cannot control their wealth (except for widows and unmarried women), the committee, unable to go to them, will inform them that they will find a special book at the central committee's office for them to inscribe their names and donations.

35. I repeat, the central committee would be committing a *huge*

mistake if it neglected to attract the sympathy of all social classes to the Workers' Union.

D. On the Use of Funds

36. The initial funds from memberships will be used: (*a*) to pay the expenses incurred by purchasing the ledgers and other small costs of that kind, (*b*) to rent premises and furnish them very simply to give the central committee a meeting place, (*c*) to cover the costs of all that is deemed useful, (*d*) to give the envoys the amount necessary for their travel, (*e*) to pay the tutors, (*f*) to allocate an amount for the defender, (*g*) to buy property measuring 100–150 hectares, (*h*) for the construction of the first palace, (*i*) to furnish it, (*j*) to cover one year's general expenses.

37. The land to be bought must, first, be located near the central committee's headquarters. For reasons of public health, it must not be more than eight kilometers away, and for the sake of convenience not more than twenty-four kilometers.[13] And second, it must be on a pretty, airy, and healthy site with very good soil. Third, it must have running water.

E. Building the Palaces

38. We have reached an era in which the social state is progressively moving toward a complete transformation. The construction of the Workers' Union palaces does not have to be solid enough to last centuries. The essential thing is that the palaces be built so as to offer simultaneously: (*a*) healthfulness in terms of space, daylight, sunniness, ventilation, and heating, (*b*) convenience in terms of ease and rapidity of communication among the different parts of the buildings, (*c*) interior: practical distribution of rooms for the elderly, employees, and children, (*d*) outside: workshops, schools, exercise rooms, and finally a farm to meet

agricultural needs. It is urgent that the palace be fed by lots of water in order always to maintain strict cleanliness. The palace architecture must be noble but simple. With its high style and ornamental beauty, it must present an aesthetic whole, harmonious in all its parts. The architect must constantly keep in mind that the children raised in these palaces are destined some day to build palaces themselves to house humankind, that they are to become *artist-artisans*, and that at a young age their hearts, imaginations, and senses must be impressed to attain that goal. Nothing will succeed better in arousing in them a taste for the arts and a passion for beauty than living in the midst of an assemblage of beautiful lines and being visually impressed by its elegance and nobility.

39. The first palace is intended as a trial; its construction ought to capture the central committee's attention.

40. Few architects can be involved in the construction. Constructing a temple, a church, a mosque, a pantheon to lodge any abstraction, or a tomb is like carving a beautiful piece of poetry in stone. To raise a palace for a prince is to write an ode; to build an asylum for 3,000 infirm, regimented soldiers is like, above all, doing a mathematical calculation. Finally, building a monastery for 1,200 monks, a hospital for 4,000 patients, barracks for 2,000 soldiers, a prison for 3,000 prisoners, or a school for 2,000 pupils—all these individuals being subject to a uniform rule—though difficult, does not require much imaginative effort on the part of the architect; whereas the *creation* of a Workers' Union palace presents serious difficulties of another sort.

41. Until now communal dwellings have been so invariably similar, to the extent of being tedious and boring, that the simple idea of living in one of the houses is most repugnant. The system of parceling estates is due to this abhorrence of communal dwellings. Thus it is essential that the Workers' Union palace look like nothing built up to now.

42. Staying at the Union palace must be pleasant and desirable; it must provoke envy just as the convent, barracks, hospital, and school provoke repugnance and disgust. Now, I can conceive of a pleasant stay only in a place where every person enjoys the well-being, activity, and rest dictated by his age, and especially a great amount of freedom. Since each of these palaces must provide shelter for two to three thousand individuals of different sexes, ages, trades, and tastes, everyone must be able to move about as much as possible without bothering his neighbor; and that is the enormous difficulty. Then, it must be realized that the Workers' Union palaces will be big centers of activity. There will be manufacturing, agriculture, moral and vocational instruction for the children, recreational activities as rewards, and relaxation for all the workers. The construction of these palaces must satisfy at the same time the needs of domestic living and the workplace, as well as the very numerous and diverse needs of farm work. It is not just a question of simply building a residence, a factory, and a farm; the three must be combined so as to create a unit. In effect, the three make up the same body, and this body must be beautiful and well proportioned. The architect will have to establish most carefully and determine most precisely the relationships to combine these three constructions into one; and if he wants the whole to be perfectly harmonious, he will have to develop each part completely. Thus, the construction of a vast communal dwelling, both tripartite and unified, fulfilling all the conditions of beauty, comfort and freedom, and capable of satisfying such diverse needs, appears to me to be an important problem to be solved. I know only one architect capable of drawing up the plan for the Workers' Union palace, and he is César Daly. Besides, he has excellent credentials; he has already made the plan for a no less difficult edifice, the small children's phalange, in accordance with Fourier's ideas. The blueprints are on display at the *Phalange* office; the central committee could go and examine them.

F. Conditions for Admission to the Palaces for the Elderly, the Injured, and Children

43. In everything beginnings inevitably present huge difficulties; Christianity took centuries to get established and be accepted. But is this to say that just because something presents great difficulty, it must not be attempted? On the contrary, the more difficulties to be overcome, the more one must hasten to begin. It will not be the same for the Workers' Union. Within ten years of its establishment it will be strong and powerful, and everything coming from it will be done with the order and care appropriate for any organization acting in accord with its constitution. The *monitors* (that is what I call those who will lead the popular and moral force) will have a very difficult mission for the first few years. It will not be possible to proceed as completely as desired.

44. Assume that the first palace has been built, furnished, and stocked for one year. The central committee will then consider admission, not according to seniority as will be done later on, but according to the funds available.

45. First, individuals will be admitted to the Union palace by department in proportion to the number of subscribers. To avoid preferences, special passes, and unfairness, straws could be drawn from a hat.

46. For instance, 600, 1,000, 1,500, or 2,000 persons will be admitted. Then as the resources increase, new palaces will be built. At this rate, in thirty years all working men and women will be sure of having their children raised in Union palaces and of finding a bed for their old age.

47. As a general rule, half those admitted will be children (entrance age will be six years) and the other half elderly or disabled.

48. I neither want nor can set a rule for admission; these regulations will change as the Union's resources grow. I believe, how-

ever, that preference ought to be given to orphans, sons of widows, or those whose parents are disabled or very old, and finally, for any worker's family with more than five children; the sixth, seventh, eighth, and beyond would enter automatically. As for the disabled, widows and widowers would have preference; but that is only a minor indication.

G. Labor Organization in the Palaces

49. The Workers' Union palaces will offer in every respect the most suitable milieu to try out one or several experiments in labor organization. Men, women, and children will all work. Since they will not have to worry about their material existence, they can choose to try whatever they want without hesitating.[14] But until there is agreement on the system to follow for labor organization, the central committee will institute a labor board in each palace. The board will have three, five, or seven men (depending upon the number of people in the palace) most capable in both theory and practice. It will be necessary to interest the board in the palace's prosperity, either through a share in the profits, security of retirement, admission for their children, or honorable distinctions. That is very important. As farming will also be practiced in the palaces, theoretical and especially practicing agriculturalists will belong to the board.

50. All men and women, being workers, will be obligated, according to their age, strength, and knowledge, to work part-time, under the supervision of a shop leader, who will fill the role of monitor and direct the children's groups.[15]

H. Moral, Intellectual, and Vocational Instruction to Be Given to the Children

51. The reader will understand that in order to treat questions of this magnitude, it would be necessary to write at least one

well-filled volume. But, wanting to give the workers just a little book, I have barely been able to indicate my thoughts.

52. A second board to supervise the children's education will have to be named. For the men and women on the school board, the same procedure will be followed as for the labor board.

53. To get intelligent, educated, moral men and women well attuned to the spirit of the Workers' Union, the central committee must be willing to make large sacrifices. High salaries, retirement security, the right to bring up their own children, nice housing, prestige—in a word, a lot must be given to the instructors in order to expect a lot from them.

54. In my opinion, there cannot be a healthy, true morality except when it logically follows from the belief in a good and just God, wisely, providentially, and carefully creating and guiding his creation. The morality to teach the children would consist in making them comprehend the existence of a good God and the always providential action exerted by God over all his creation. Raised in this belief from the age of six, the child would be protected from ridiculous superstition, absurd fears, and stupid prejudices that generally are the share of the masses. Then, the child would learn that the law of humanity is continuous and that perfectibility is its condition. By every means possible, the child would have to be led to understand that our globe is a large humanitarian body, whose different nations represent its internal organs, members, and main arteries and whose individuals represent the other arteries, veins, nerves, muscles, and even the tiniest fibers. All the parts of this great body are as closely connected to each other as the various parts of the human body, all helping each other and receiving life from the same source. A nerve, a muscle, a vessel, or a fiber cannot suffer without the whole body's feeling it. Similarly, when a foot, an arm, or a finger hurts, the whole body ails. Nothing is easier to teach the child than this indivisibility of the big humanitarian body and the

solidarity of nations and people. If this image has until now not been introduced in the schools, it is the fault of religious and political opinions that have divided nations and people.

55. With this image, reproduced in all its forms and at the level of the child's mentality, the children will eventually understand perfectly that in loving and serving their brothers in humanity, in the long run they serve and love themselves, and that in hating and harming their brothers in humanity, they eventually hate and harm themselves.

56. Do not come and say that such a morality would only legitimate egotism. People who think that are narrow-minded and shortsighted. Loving and serving oneself in humanity is loving and serving God's creature. And is this not what Jesus meant when he said, "Love thy neighbor as thyself"? Then, "Do unto others as you would have them do unto you. Love and serve one another." The word *religion* means banding together. Well, I ask you, how can you rally nations, peoples, and individuals around the same notion to work for a common goal, if nations, peoples, and individuals hate and kill each other? How can a Frenchman love an Englishman, a Russian, or a Turk, if he does not understand that it is in his own interest to love and serve them, because they are in it with him and he with them. If love is the soul of intelligence, intelligence in its turn is the torch of love. Together these two terms form what I shall call understanding and complete sense; whereas one without the other makes something bastard, incomplete, and castrated, without strength, power, or life.

57. By separating love from intelligence, a mortal blow was delivered to Jesus's religion. Catholicism said, "Believe and do not analyze." What is the result? Those with natures more *intelligent* than loving, the scholars and philosophers, finding no suitable nourishment for their minds in the Catholic religion, abjured the Church, heaping much disdain, distrust, and insult upon it. From disdain they moved to anger and indignation, and hitting

twice as hard, they demolished the grand edifice stone by stone. On the other hand, those who are more *loving* than intelligent, seduced by the attractive power of ecstasy, ruined and lost themselves in the emptiness. For loving God outside humanity is scornful and insulting, an outrage to God in His manifestation.

58. Thus the teachers ought to have as their fundamental law the simultaneous development of the loving and intellectual faculties of every child.

59. If one wants to obtain this double result, a very powerful element must be introduced into the method—the *why*. The Jacotot method* lies partly in posing the question, *"Why?"* Consequently, I would like to see it more widely accepted. Applying the *why* to solving great moral, social, and philosophical questions in the daily education given to children of the working class would be the way to make human intelligence take gigantic strides.

60. Thus, instead of tiring the schoolchild by making him memorize a bunch of useless things, the development of his reasoning would be the sole concern, through the study of the "whys" explained in everything. Taught in this manner, a child of twelve or thirteen could understand the reason for anything he might be asked to do, as well as, within limits, the explanation of things in general. This method of teaching is so superior to any other that a special treatise ought to be prepared to be used as the basis for all teaching in the palaces.

61. The school board would come to terms with the shop and farm directors so that all three things would operate smoothly. Fourier's works would have to be consulted.† The section in

---

* Jean-Joseph Jacotot (1770–1841) originated the "universal" method of education, which called for the student to learn on his own with no instructor to expound upon the subject matter. Tristan was probably familiar with his book, *Enseignement universel*, published in 1822.

† These works by Charles Fourier include *Théorie des quatre mouvements* (1808), *Traité de l'association domestique-agricole* (1822), and in particular *Théorie de l'unité universelle* (1822), *Le Nouveau Monde industriel et sociétaire* (1829), and *La Fausse Industrie morcelée* (1835–36).

which he treats vocational training for children contains some very good things. Leaving aside the bulk of his *system*, one can accept everything judged capable of being applied to the young pupils in the Workers' Union palace. One can do the same with Owen: adopt his educational method, which is similar to the one I am proposing (the Why).*

62. If the Workers' Union wants to create free men and women, the children must be taught to show great respect for human dignity in all aspects of life. To insure this respect, they must be taught never to harm or insult another and never to allow the least injustice or slightest insult, either on the part of their peers or on the part of their superiors. To make this more emphatic, I would like everything in the settlement to be spelled out in written laws and regulations so that the rights and duties of each would be clearly and precisely defined.

63. These printed laws and regulations would be distributed to everyone, so that only the law and never the ruler's arbitrary will is obeyed.

64. In no case might a person be subjected to degrading punishment in the palace. If a child or old person misbehaved, he would be sent away and could not return.[16]

65. As every being, respectful of himself and of others, shows it by being well groomed, it would be essential to accustom the children to taking care of themselves through extreme cleanliness. I would like the same concern to be given to their personal care as to their culture and intellect. By dint of suffering and being deprived, the masses today are quite rachitic. Well, these rickets would have to be fought with all the means available to medicine: exercise, gymnastics, etc. Receiving the child by the age of six

---

* In her final chapter in the *Promenades dans Londres* (1840), Tristan elaborates Robert Owen's pedagogical theories as they were implemented at New Lanark. While she was favorably impressed with their results, she does not completely agree with his fundamental view of human nature.

(none would be taken beyond this age) would still permit time to give him proper care for his teeth, hair, and feet. His body would be strengthened through appropriate work, and he would be given food best suited to his temperament. Various diets would have to be followed: meat and wine for some; vegetables, fruit, and water for others. The Union offers such great advantages that everything seemingly impossible to us in our individual households becomes simple in such a vast organization.

66. It will be wise to adopt a uniform fulfilling three essential conditions: (a) that its shape and material not hinder in any way the physical development of the child—for instance, the girls will not wear any corsets, the boys no suspenders or ties; (b) that it be comfortable to work in and not easily soiled; and (c) that it be elegantly cut, completely harmonious, and pleasant to look at.

67. As for vocational training, each child would choose the trade he feels the most suited for. Besides all the other work he would have to do, upon leaving the palace he will have to be a competent worker in at least two trades.

68. In order for him to become interested in work, as of the age of ten the child will be eligible to share in the profits produced by the work in the establishment. This amount will increase every year until his departure at the age of eighteen. Half will be given to him as a trousseau made in the establishment and the other half in money.

69. Boarders could perhaps be taken in and put to the same conditions as the union children. Between the ages of six and ten, they would receive their share in the work profits. The bourgeoisie would not hesitate to take advantage of such conditions for their children. Small investors, small businessmen, unsuccessful artists, etc., would be delighted to be able to place their children and only have to pay for four years of board (knowing that they would be well brought up and given a state in life). I am offering this idea because I think it is possible and could be useful to the petty bourgeois, who must be attracted to the cause of the work-

ing class by all possible benefits. This, like the rest, is only in rough-draft form and merits further examination.

70. As an act of high religiosity, I would also like each palace to offer its hospitality to a dozen persons (six men and six women) who would have as their title *palace guests*. They would be selected from among elderly (not to be admitted before the age of sixty) artists, professors, scholars, and writers lacking resources. Foreigners would receive preferential treatment. The guests would occupy seats of honor at all the ceremonies; this would be morality in action, to teach children respect for talent even when its circumstances are impoverished. The presence of the twelve guests treated with respect and consideration would make a greater impression on the child used to reverently greeting the stranger than all the beautiful harangues in verse and prose produced by our poets and novelists about the respect due to misfortune, talent, age, etc.

I. The Inevitable Results of This Education

71. The results the Workers' Union ought to have are immeasurable. This union is a bridge erected between a dying civilization and the harmonious social order foreseen by superior minds. First of all, it will bring about the rehabilitation of manual labor diminished by thousands of years of slavery. And this is a capital point. As soon as it is no longer dishonorable to work with one's hands, when work is even an honorable deed,[17] the rich and the poor alike will work. For idleness is both a torture for mankind and the cause of its ills. All will work, and for this reason alone, prosperity will rule for everyone. Then, there will be no more poverty; and poverty ceasing, ignorance will too. Who causes the evil we suffer from today? Isn't it that thousand-headed monster, *selfishness?* But selfishness is not the primary cause; poverty and ignorance are what produce selfishness.

72. Suppose a peasant has an abundance of plums in his garden and the same is true for his neighbors, so that no one comes to buy them. In this case, the peasant will be very charitable: he will let the poor from the village eat his plums. But let a railroad be built through the same village situated thirty leagues from the capitol, so that the peasant can cheaply transport his plums to Paris where they will sell for twelve francs a bushel. Oh, then will our fellow change his tune regarding the poor! Cursed be he who passes by the tree and dares pick a plum; the peasant will spend day and night watching over his property. He will shout "Thief!" if his sacred rights are attacked! And he will pitilessly press charges against the guilty old beggar for having picked a plum. Without remorse or shame, he will have him put in jail for the theft, because that plum represents a half-farthing. Will it be said, "There's a very selfish peasant"? Not at all; and the proof that this man was not born selfish is that, when he had too many plums for himself, he gave the excess to the poor. Should the railroad be extended another hundred leagues and so many plums arrive in Paris that they sell only for fifty cents a bushel, then you will see this same peasant stop being selfish and let the poor take his plums. Society is in exactly the same position as the peasant; it is selfish because it is poor in productivity. If tomorrow it were to produce an abundance of everything, selfishness would disappear.

73. Only when all men and women work with their hands and are dignified by it, will this great, desirable productivity take place. And this is the only way to eradicate the vices fostered by selfishness, and consequently to civilize men.

74. The second, but not lesser, result necessarily brought about by the Workers' Union will be to establish de facto real equality among all men. In fact, as soon as the day comes when working-class children are carefully raised and trained to develop their intellects, faculties, and physical strength—in a word, all that is good and beautiful in human nature—and as soon as there is no

distinction between rich and poor children in their education, talent, and good manners, I ask: where could there be inequality? Nowhere, absolutely nowhere. Then only one inequality will be recognized, but that one must be experienced and accepted, for God is the One who established it. To one, he gives genius, love, intelligence, wit, strength, and beauty; to the other, he denies all these gifts and makes him stupid, dull-minded, weak-bodied, and ill-shapen. That is natural inequality before which man's pride must humble itself; that inequality indiscriminately touches the sons of kings as well as the sons of the poor.

75. I stop here, wanting to leave my readers the sweet joy of counting for themselves the important and magnificent results the Workers' Union will doubtless obtain. In this institution the country will find elements of order, prosperity, wealth, morality, and happiness, such as they can be desired.

NOTES

1. The societies in Paris and the suburbs number 236, with 15,840 subscribers and about three million francs in funds (*De la Condition des ouvriers de Paris de 1789 jusqu'en 1841*, p. 254).

2. If I am not allowing for an equal number of men and women on the committees, it is because it has been observed that today's working women are much less educated and intellectually less developed than the male workers. But of course this inequality will only be transitory.

3. The Workers' Union, proceeding in the name of *universal unity*, must not make any distinction between nationalities or male and female workers belonging to whichever nation on earth. Therefore, for anyone called a foreigner, the Union benefits will be absolutely the same as for the French.

The Workers' Union will have to set up branch committees in all the main towns in England, Germany, and Italy—in a word, in all the European capitols—so that men and women workers of all the European nations can be listed in the Workers' Union register as members. The same steps will have to be taken for these committees as for the French ones. The membership contributions will be sent to the central committee, and each Union member will have the right for himself to be admitted, or in turn, for his children.

4. In Paris there are 275,000 workers of all ages and both sexes. To this should be added 50,000 for the porters, their wives and children, servants of both sexes, and messengers. Men and women who do laundry and sewing at home or as day-workers can be put at 50,000. All told, this makes 335,000 to 350,000 workers (*De la Condition des ouvriers de Paris*, p. 234).

5. Certain people will be dismayed at the idea of gathering fourteen million with small contributions of two francs. Yet, nothing would be simpler than for *steady* workers (easily half can be counted in this group), employed by order-loving employers who understand that the country's prosperity depends upon the well-being of the working class (and let us say it, these employers are in the majority), to agree with their employers that they would each contribute two francs to the Workers' Union collectors. Then there would be no problem for either the worker or the collector. As for the workers not regularly employed by the same employers, their membership contributions clearly cannot be made as easily and will be a greater problem for the collectors; but, in the long run, it is feasible.

Besides, in this regard, one can be guided by what O'Connell and the steering committee set up in Ireland, and there collecting presents much greater difficulties since they are paid one cent per week. The religious societies have established these kinds of contributions everywhere; the faithful give one cent per week, six cents per month, etc. All these small amounts, with which priests of all the religions do so much, are gathered either by members of the brotherhoods or by some priest, without the least difficulty.

6. The head-town will be the one with the most workers.

7. As the provinces almost always owe money to Paris, Paris will tend to stay in the black.

8. The dictionary defines *King* (from the Latin *rex*, *regis*, derived from *regere*, to rule, to govern) as the one who exercises

sovereign power in a kingdom and *leader* as the one who is at the head, who commands, directs, leads, etc.

9. Louis-Philippe, elected King of the French on August 9, 1830.

10. Queen Elizabeth I gave her palace at Greenwich to be made into a hospital for sailors.

11. What women can do when they want can be judged by what has just occurred regarding the disaster in Pointe-à-Pitre. With the Queen at their head, all the great ladies of the Court went to work *with their hands* and with unbelievable activity. They organized collections and lotteries, and we even saw them become shopkeepers for charity! (See the *Journal des Débats*, April 30, 1842). [Tristan is referring to the 1836–37 eruptions of the volcano *La Soufrière* in Guadeloupe.—*Trans.*]

12. The color *white* (for *unity*) ought to be adopted by the Workers' Union for their flag. Its slogan will be: *Workers' Union for the right to work and to organize.*

13. By rail, this distance represents only one half-hour.

14. Provided, however, that the means do not jeopardize human freedom and dignity, as, for example, the regimentation proposed by Monsieur Enfantin.

15. I hope that no one will be tempted to distort my thought and accuse me of trying to create workhouses under the name of palaces or asylums for beggars where the poor are forced into drudgery. The elderly and the children, to the extent that the doctors judge them able, will do physical work for two, four, or five hours a day, but never on any occasion for more than six hours a day—and the work will have to be varied so as to be pleasurable rather than tedious.

16. The seriousness of the cases would be determined by established guidelines.

17. I am totally of Fourier's opinion that a means must be found to make work *attractive;* but I think that before reaching this ultimate goal, work must first cease being considered *dishonorable.*

Summary of the ideas in this book, the goals of which are:

1. Consolidation of the working class by means of a tight, solid, and indissoluble Union.

2. Representation of the working class before the nation through a defender chosen and paid by the Workers' Union, so that the working class's need to exist and the other classes' need to accept it become evident.

3. Recognition of one's hands as legitimate property. (In France 25,000,000 proletarians have their hands as their only asset.)

4. Recognition of the legitimacy of the right to work for all men and women.

5. Recognition of the legitimacy of the right to moral, intellectual, and vocational education for all boys and girls.

6. Examination of the possibility of labor organizing in the current social state.

7. Construction of Workers' Union palaces in every department, in which working-class children would receive intellectual and vocational instruction, and to which the infirm and elderly as well as workers injured on the job would be admitted.

8. Recognition of the urgent necessity of giving moral, intellectual, and vocational education to the women of the masses so that they can become the moral agents for the men of the masses.

9. Recognition in principle of equal rights for men and women as the sole means of unifying humankind.

Appeal to the Workers

Working men and women,

In your name and in view of your well-being and your common happiness I come, my brothers and sisters, to ask your help and support to build the first *palace* to receive your young children, your poor brothers injured at work, and your elderly fathers exhausted from fatigue.

May all of you who feel a spark of love in your hearts unite your generous efforts and cooperate, each according to his means, in the prompt realization of this great work!

And you, Agricol Perdiguier, guild historian and reformer; you, Pierre Moreau, the bold renovator; you, Gosset, the father of blacksmiths, improver of guilds; you, Vinçard, author-poet-songwriter; you, Poncy, Savinien Lapointe, Ponty, Duquenne, Durand, Rolly, etc., etc.*

* For Perdiguier, Moreau, and Gosset, see p. 45. Jules Vinçard (1796–1879) was the official "liturgical" poet for the Saint-Simonians; he co-authored *La Foi nouvelle* (1831) and wrote *Mémoires épisodiques d'un chansonnier saint-simonien* (1878). Charles Poncy (1821–91), a mason, published his *Poésies* in 1840, *Marines* (1842), *Le Chantier* with a preface by George Sand (1844), and *Chansons pour chaque métier* (1850). Savinien Lapointe (1811–93), a shoemaker and Saint-Simonian, wrote *Une Voix d'en-bas* (1844), *Echos de la rue* (1852), and a five-act tragedy entitled *Les Juifs sous Charles VI*; he received encouragement from the likes of Victor Hugo, George Sand, and Béranger. Louis Ponty (1803–79), who became a Saint-Simonian, wrote many poems and songs and was published in Rodrigues's anthology. Alexis Durand was a cabinetmaker and poet from Fontainebleau. Michel Roly (not Rolly), a Parisian cabinetmaker and poet, also published in Rodrigues's anthology.

You, Elisa Moreau, Louise Crombach, Antoinette Quarré, Marie Carpentier, Elisa Fleury, etc.*

You, the editors of *La Ruche*, *L'Atelier*, *le Populaire*, *L'Artisan*, *Le Nouveau Monde*, *Le Travail*, etc.†

Finally all of you, worker-poets, writers, speakers, musicians, intelligent and well-intentioned men and women, I hereby solemnly appeal to you. In the name of your divided and unhappy brothers, in the name of love for humanity, and in your own names, I call on you to preach through speaking and writing: *The universal union of working men and women*.

So to work! To work, my brothers. The work will be rough, the difficulties numerous, but think of the greatness of the goal! The greatness of the reward!

Through you, the unification of human kind.

* Elise (not Elisa) Moreau (b. 1813) wrote *Rêves d'une jeune fille* (1832), among other works. Antoinette Quarré (1813–47), a hunchbacked seamstress, was patronized by the master poet Lamartine. Tristan went to see her in Dijon on April 19, 1844, and recorded in her journal: "Instinctively I have a strong dislike for everything ugly, and I must say, experience and study have come to confirm what this instinct had shown me. . . . After a few moments of conversation with Mademoiselle Antoinette Quarré, everything she said proved to me that internally she corresponded perfectly with her appearance" (*Le Tour*, p. 45). Marie Carpentier, from Sarthe, wrote *Préludes*. Elisa Fleury, an embroiderer, contributed to Rodrigues's anthology.

† *La Ruche populaire* was edited by a group of workers of whom Jules Vinçard's nephew Pierre (1820–82) was among the more active. *L'Atelier* (1840–50) was managed by Leneveux. *Le Populaire* was Etienne Cabet's journal. Tristan heavily criticized Cabet and his Icarian school in her journal (*Le Tour*, p. 86). *L'Artisan* saw only four issues in September-October 1830. *Le Nouveau Monde* was edited by Jean Czynski and *Le Travail* by Moreau-Christophe (1799–1881), who also wrote an exposé of British prisons (which Tristan quotes in her *Promenades dans Londres*, ch. IX).

Advice to the Workers

Workers, if you want to leave behind your state of poverty, become educated.

Those among you who read, generally read terrible books. Habits must be changed: instead of spending your money on songs, "pittoresques," "physiologies,"* and a hodge-podge of nonsense without any useful information, buy *good books*.

"But good books are expensive," you will tell me, "and we have no money." Unite, and then you will be rich.

If you want to put together a little library of a dozen or so good works (no more are needed), why don't you form small associations? For example, twelve, fifteen, or twenty workers, men and women, who know each other and live in the same neighborhood, could get together and do this. With a small membership fee the twelve works could be purchased and would belong in common to the association members. Just think—with *unity* miracles can be made!

In the event you accept this idea, I am going to mention the works it would be good for you to read and reread every Sunday. They should be studied, commented upon and discussed among you, in a word, *known thoroughly*, absolutely as the Jews know their Bible and the Catholics their prayer book. In France one proceeds so superficially that people will tell you, "I leafed through

* By "pittoresques," Tristan is probably referring to picture books. "Physiologies," a literary genre in style during the first part of the nineteenth century (e.g. Balzac's *Physiologie du mariage*), were intended to be objective descriptions of some human reality. Tristan probably objected to the ones which passed as "objective" but catered to more sensational interests.

through that book; I know it." This ridiculous presumptuousness is what makes the French know everything but understand nothing.

The first title on the list is by Eugène Buret, *De la Misère des classes laborieuses en Angleterre et en France*. In this work you will find a frightening but truthful picture of the poverty and moral degradation into which the working class has fallen in England and France. Although this book is very painful, you must have the courage to read it, for it is essential to know exactly what your situation is. Otherwise you will make no effort to get out of it. Also study Monsieur Frégier's work, *Des Classes dangereuses dans la ville de Paris;* the one by Monsieur Villermé, *Des Prisons de France;* the one by Parent-Duchâtelet, *De la Prostitution dans la ville de Paris;* the one by Gustave de Beaumont, *l'Irlande religieuse, morale et politique*. And at last, putting all false modesty aside, I take the liberty of mentioning my *Promenades dans Londres*. I wrote this book to instruct the workers; thus I naturally want very much to see it filter into the working classes. Also buy Louis Blanc's little book, *L'Organisation du travail;* Monsieur Proudhon's *La Célébration du dimanche;* the work by Adolphe Boyer, *De l'Etat des ouvriers;* the book on the guild system by Agricol Perdiguier; Gosset's little pamphlet also on the same question; and Pierre Moreau's second work, *De la Réforme des abus du compagnonnage et de l'Amélioration du sort des travailleurs*.[1]

NOTE

1. To my great regret, I cannot suggest here any work by Fourier or the Societarian School as suitable for the workers. Until now, Fourier's doctrine has not been accessible to workers; it would be something great to do. Let us hope that the leaders of the Societarian School will finally understand the urgency and absolute necessity of bringing out an edition of their master's work that can be understood by the public. In my opinion, that is the only way to convey Fourier's power and vitality.

To the Bourgeois

During times of egotism and blindness like the one we live in, when demanding rights for the most populous class one cannot be too cautious about protection against slander and violent attacks by unintelligent or evil people. This is why I have judged it wise and prudent to direct a few words here to the gentlemen of the bourgeoisie. I want them to realize that I am not a revolutionary or an anarchist or a bloodthirsty person. (I shall spare my readers the litany of more or less frightening epithets which certain bourgeois are in the ridiculous habit of using in such circumstances.)

But before absolving myself of the absurd accusations I expect to receive,[1] I must state that I see the bourgeois in two categories. Today the bourgeoisie is divided into two distinct camps. On one side are the blind and deaf; the cripples might even be added. For just as in Christ's time, they have eyes and cannot see; ears and cannot hear; legs and cannot walk. In this camp the deaf do not hear the great but varied humanitarian voice crying out that the time has come for there to be no more outcasts on earth, when every individual, upon his entrance into life, must have, as a member of the great human family, his seat at the social banquet. In this camp the blind do not see the large movement forming from top to bottom. In this camp those crippled by their total inertia let the others go ahead without noticing they remain behind. All these poor ailing creatures are like laggards abandoned by an army corps because they bother and hamper the march.

On the other side are the intelligent bourgeois. I shall call them the sighted ones. In the sighted camp, one is moved with love in hearing the great humanitarian voice vibrate and cry out, "Brothers, give us room!" In the sighted camp, one can clearly perceive the great ascending movement of the lower classes gradually moving up step by step toward well-being and freedom. This march is followed with interest and concern. With the sighted ones, the march is endless—in thought, in work, and through the impulse *of generous sympathy.*

The sighted bourgeois are today the ones who form the reason, wisdom, and strength of the nation. If unfortunately it happens, as it must be feared, that the blind compromise the nation's interests through their blunders, the country will find intelligent, good, firm, and able men in the sighted camp to save France once again.

Therefore I am not speaking to the sighted ones here; that would be insulting to them. Besides, I myself belong to this camp. Our slogan is this: order and respect for all kinds of property; justice for all; general wealth and prosperity for the country.

With that said, I beg the deaf bourgeois to be willing to reflect soundly, if possible, upon my idea, before distorting and slandering my intentions. Here is precisely the essence of my thought:

Instinctively, religiously and systematically, I love and want justice. I love and want order. This love emanating from our Creator and breathing life into every creature's soul makes me understand the solidarity that unites the individual with everything. I want justice for all, because of justice is born general order, and of general order are born well-being, wealth, security, and productive activity; and that is happiness.

Solely in view of *order* do I want the working class to demand its right to work and its right to moral and vocational education, because increased productivity necessarily depends upon their degree of education; and the country's wealth and prosperity obviously depend upon the labor of the most populous class. I want the working class to make its demands in the name of rights, so that there is no need to demand in the name of force.

Instinctively, religiously, and systematically, I am protesting against everything obtained by brute force; I do not want society to be exposed to suffering from brute force left in the hands of the people any more than I want it to suffer from brute force placed in the hands of power. In both cases, there would be injustice, and consequently disorder.

If the people are denied the right to education and the right to work, what will happen? Embittered by suffering and aroused by reading about the horror of their position without any indication of how to better it,[2] the people will become more and more brutal, crude, vicious, and wicked. In this state they will become a formidable enemy for the rich classes, and public security as well as the country's prosperity will be in constant jeopardy. Who wouldn't be afraid to imagine the horrible unrest produced by hatred and animosity in a country where ten to twelve million uneducated workers have no moral direction or guarantee of jobs? Deserted in this way, the workers would become a redoubtable group in French society which could be led by the first political intriguer who came along to upset the order. Just like the slaves in Roman society, the workers would join forces with Catiline and attack society.*

Yes, I ask that the working class be unified in one body and have representation in the Chamber; and though certain retrogressive minds may find this measure very revolutionary, I maintain and shall prove that it is, on the contrary, a measure in favor of *order*.

Suffering, deserted, and leaderless, the workers are in exactly the same position as a man afflicted with a grave illness without a doctor to tend to him. In this cruel situation the patient worries, agitates, and takes any medicine the first charlatan passing along offers him. Instead of relieving his ailment, these remedies aggravate it; and the more he suffers and is weakened, the more the charlatans appear with their drugs. The people are in just that

* Catiline (Lucius Sergius Catalina) plotted against the Roman Senate and was denounced by Cicero in 63 B.C.

situation. If they are not allowed to choose a legal defender, an honest, dedicated, and conscientious man to defend their interests and demand their rights, what will happen? Intriguers from all parties will come and propose to defend them, creating illegal secret societies whose members, as we have seen since 1830, are duped and victimized by a few political leaders unconcerned with the true interest of the people.* From these societies emerge plots, riots, and assassinations. Public order is disturbed and the country's prosperity suffers. The national leadership is frightened, and, out of fear, they pass anti-terror laws that aggravate the problem. Then disorder, grief, misery, and suffering for everyone arise out of the brutality and injustice on both sides. This is the tale of what has happened since 1789. Let us now suppose that the people are granted what I am requesting—a defender. Then, no more secret societies and no more riots. As soon as the people know that an honorable man is in charge of defending them and he actively goes about it, they will calm down and wait patiently.[3]

To ask for a defender for the working class is to want to replace the anonymous charlatans by a well-known university doctor; it is the desire to substitute brute force with the right to rule. To grant the working class the right to choose a defender worthy of its cause from among honorable men would be an act of prudence and order. The publisher of *La Revue Indépendante* will, I think, revoke his poorly thought-out opinion, or at least he will be the only one, I hope, to envisage the Workers' Union defender as a mercenary hired simply to overthrow the government. If Monsieur Pernet were among the sighted ones, he would understand that there would be no advantage for the workers in overthrowing the government. Since 1789 lots of governments have been toppled, and what have the workers gained from these revolutions: Aren't they always carried out at their own expense? Aren't *they*

* The secret societies that formed in the early 1830s included anticlerical petty bourgeois who opposed the devout upper bourgeoisie.

the ones who fight? Aren't *they* the ones who are killed? And then after the tumult follows disorder; capital funds are retracted; business lags; there is no work; and the worker starves to death. What a lovely advantage for him in making revolutions! No sirs, I do not want the workers to hire a revolutionary, a perturber of the public peace. Far from that; I want them to pay generously a man of heart and talent to prevent revolutions, because revolutions turn against the freedom and true interests of the people.

I have just expressed the exact truth on my feelings here. Now, if it pleases the deaf and blind to cry scandal before my revolutionary doctrines, then I can only say, "My Lord, forgive them, for they know not what they do."

NOTES

1. Monsieur Pagnerre and the "friends of the people" are not the only ones to act in contradiction to their reputations. When a journal has as its title *Revue Indépendante* (Independent Review), it ought to be completely independent concerning serious issues. So I thought that, in accordance with its title, the editor would be independent enough to include a chapter from my work, as did *La Phalange* (cf. the issues of March 29 and 31, 1845). Therefore I wrote to Monsieur Pernet, the editor of the *Revue Indépendante*, to ask him to accept an excerpt from the work I was about to publish. But to my surprise and stupefaction, his reply accused me of being a *revolutionary*, of wanting to subsidize the overturn of the government, etc.

The *Journal des Débats*, at the time of its most furious outbursts, would not have been so harsh. And to think that such accusations are coming from the editor of the *only* democratic review that remains. It is beyond belief; so I must present a passage from that strange letter:

". . . Your union plan is basically nothing more than a political association. Isn't it clear that collecting memberships to subsidize the upheaval of the current economic order and charging fees and gathering to have the press give out revolutionary propaganda, instruction, and preachings are all ploys of politics and agitation against the established government? Begin by abolishing the law on associations and then you will be able to promote your union plan. Until then, no matter how excellent or practical, all projects of this kind will be nothing more than utopias. The government pursued the completely commercial association of the St. Etienne ribbon-makers. Thus all the more reason why it would not allow an association even more threatening in its goal and breadth."

The letter was such as to give me serious doubts about how my ideas were going to be understood. If the editor of the *Revue Indépendante*, the "most advanced" expression (according to its label) of our times, accused me of being an anarchist, my goodness, what would those short-sighted conservatives say! Monsieur Pernet's letter made me understand that I have to explain my intentions frankly and clearly. His inconceivable charges are the determining factor in this address to the bourgeois.

2. The works of Lamennais and so many others on the same order of ideas.

3. See Gustave de Beaumont's work on Ireland for what he reports on this subject. Before O'Connell took up the defense of the Irish cause, there had been revolutions in Ireland *every six months*. And with each revolution, the English government reacted by tightening the chains of the unfortunate still more, so that their attempts at emancipation left them more violently enslaved through brute force.

Letter and Song by Charles Poncy

I had requested a song from Monsieur Poncy, and he sent me one. The letter with it adds new merit to this precious gift. It proves that the poet is *really a mason* and that the *mason is a great poet*.

Madame,

I ask you please to forgive my long delay in answering you. But I work three leagues from town on an island where we are building a quarantine station. There, I live far from any literature, politics, or current news. I live with a few Genoans, the sky, and the sea. That is all. Furthermore, I work like a damned man all day long, and manual labor leaves me only brief moments of leisure in the evening for my literary work, happy as I am when sleep doesn't destroy them. Letters reach me only by cargo boat, often more than two weeks after they arrive in Toulon. This is what happened with yours. Here is my work; I am already convinced that it will not please you. You didn't want a *chant* from me, but a song: the Workers' Union *Marseillaise*. I don't know how to write songs. When I tried, I wrote uneven verse, and the rhymes were ridiculous. Vinçard would have done this Union song a thousand times better than I. Nevertheless, I wanted to prove my willingness to be agreeable to you and useful to my brothers.

Charles Poncy

THE UNION

To the People

My brothers, it is time that hatreds be forgot;
For all peoples to rally under a single flag!
The salvation road is going to be laid out for us.
The great freedom humanity dreams of
Like a new radiant sun is rising
   On the horizon of the future.

So that this sun of clarity inundates us;
So that each day its divine fire inspires
Our hearts, where the Eternal sowed the truth;
We must complete the work God begins;
Our sweat and immense love must
   Engender brotherhood!

The UNION must maintain your flame;
Oh, people! harbor its banner in the eyes of all!
. . . .
Be united. The UNION will give you strength,
   And strength, freedom.

The UNION, harmony, here everything comes from them!
Oh, my brothers! See the poor swallows,
On the wings of spring return toward our skies!
See how much love these sweet birds harbor,
So that together they support each other over the Ocean,
   When the tempest breaks upon them!

What matter the lightning, axes, and thunder,
To those great woods filled with centenary oaks?

On their dense trunks the South winds break;
And these vast forests, as old as the world,
Defying the winter wind which trims them,
   Turn green every Spring.

Look when the sea wants to pull back its shores!
It evokes the savage squadrons with its waves
The waves, when called, proudly rush,
Against the dark cliff they all fall together,
And under their powerful slap the chain of rocks trembles
   And the second time crumbles.

Again, see the flowers, the poor flowers of the plains,
Their corollas are full of honey and perfume;
Their cups live on air, dew, and love.
A halo shines for a long time on their faces,
While each flower, isolating itself from its sisters,
   Is born and dies, gone in a day.

Oh, my brothers! Let's follow these sublime models.
Let us unite our efforts like the swallows,
Like the woods, the waves, and the poor flowers;
Let us unite our skiffs to cross life,
That stormy sea where every soul is followed
   By a long cortege of grief.

May our hearts, enlightened by these powerful examples,
Adore the UNION and become its temples!
The people are on the threshold of coming into their own.
The rights taken away are yet to be reclaimed;
But the HOLY UNION is there to give us back all;
   Glory, happiness, and liberty!

Brothers, let us strike up the hymn of harmony,
Let every voice be in tune with our inspired chants.
Our glorious efforts will be blessed by God.
From the sunset plains to those of dawn,
A thousand echoes will reply from the four corners of the earth:
   Let's be united! Let's be united!

Charles Poncy, mason

Several pieces of poetry and *The Workers' Union Marseillaise* were sent to me by workers, students, and women.

Here I give the two songs that received the most votes.

I had also made an appeal to composers and conducted a contest. All the compositions sent in were submitted to a musical jury. The composition by Monsieur A. Thys obtained the majority of votes and he won the prize. The prize is a gold medal donated by Eugène Sue.*

* There were four entries in the contest; Poncy's song arrived too late for the judging, which Béranger was supposed to supervise. The "Songwriters Guild" constituted the musical jury. See Dominique Desanti, *A Woman in Revolt: A Biography of Flora Tristan*, translated by Elizabeth Zelvin (New York: Crown, 1976), p. 228.

The Workshop Marseillaise. Music by Thys, words by Gallinove.

THE WORKSHOP MARSEILLAISE

To the Workers

Branches of the people's oak,
To grow, let us unite our efforts:
Beneath the storm of misery
Let us unite to be strong.
   The most noble head
Soon bends under the angry sky;
To rise in defying the storm,
   Let us unite, let us unite!   (Repeat)

Without an intelligent head
Every great body perishes voiceless:
May a man with an eloquent voice
Come and demand our rights!
   To the scolding pride
He will reply without bending a knee;
To foster the world's deputy,
   Let us unite, let us unite!   (Repeat)

Others have shares in gold,
Names, crests, contracts:
Labor is our heritage,
And our titles are our hands.
   All have the right to live:
For nature gives life to all:
But for labor finally to free us,
   Let us unite, let us unite.   (Repeat)

Let us give alms to all the world:
Love for us is a treasure.

And without shaking any throne,
Make gold from our coins.
   Each one is a stone,
And the palace will grow for all,
Let us give hope for the worker family,
   Let us unite, let us unite!   (Repeat)

You who are outraged by a brutal ardor,
Your rights will rule in their turn,
We shall make your share equal,
And you will return with love for our hearts.
   Your choice is free,
Women, our sisters, your heart is yours.
Let us put marriage in a just balance,
   Let us unite, let us unite.   (Repeat)

Thus speaks a new voice,
To whom our hearts have opened:
And the humanity it is calling
Awakens and blushes with its strength.
   But let us reject the sword . . .
Peace is reborn, the sky becomes calmer . . .
To greet the great day which is rising,
   Let us unite, let us unite!   (Repeat)

Gallinove, painter

THE WORKERS' UNION MARSEILLAISE

Glory to work, glory to love
Through which all men are brothers,
And may heaven hasten the day
For our workers' rights!
Let us unite; in unity
Will disappear our slavery,
And from disinherited people
We will be reborn a wise people!

Old flags, tossed by the winds of chance,
  Give in to the unity that founds
And you, Christ's spirit, under the same banner
  Rally the soldiers of the world!

Surge forth, noble defender,
Magnanimous and powerful brother,
You, a leader without fear, will make
The faith motivating us speak!
Interpreter of our hundred voices,
To the tribunal of France
Ascend: and demanding our rights,
Immortalize your eloquence!

Old flags, etc.

Slumber amidst the vanities,
Thesaurizers of power,
Without attacking your liberties,
We proclaim our alliance.
Come! Your sumptuous palaces
Will lack the stony brilliance
Of the majestic monuments,
Palaces of the working class!

Old flags, etc.

All our rights of man are yours,
Oh, mothers of humanity,
On your faces as on ours is needed
The sun of equality!
Upon this new world star
Place your triumphant gaze,
Oh, women, the fecund blood
Is attested by your children!

Old flags, etc.

Leclair, student

Project for a Weekly Journal Entitled "The Workers' Union," Specifically Intended for Workers[1]

The more I study the working class and research the *cause* of its abuses, the more convinced I remain that, in the moral as in the physical world, evil comes solely from *ignorance*. Therefore, whatever the price, the working class must be extracted from this state of ignorance unless one wants to risk the country's future.

To fight the enemy (ignorance), one of the most effective means would be to create an organ written by men of heart and intelligence, who love justice and consequently their fellow man. I am certain some generous souls might still be found to work hard and conscientiously on such a project.

The journal I have conceived of would have as its goal:

1. To represent and instruct the most populous, the most useful, the strongest and most important part of the nation in its rights, duties, and interests (thirty million proletarians against, at most, four million employers).

2. To make known the suffering, needs, and interests of these thirty million proletarians and to do this only in view of improvement and happiness for *all men* and *women*, rich and poor.

3. To demand social and political rights for thirty million proletarians, always in the country's general interest and by peaceful and legal means.

The proletarian class, that is to say, indeed *the nation*, has been up to now so deserted and scorned and has remained so truly nil in the political and social movement that it does not yet have a serious organ whose special mission would be to represent it, demand its rights, and defend its interests. I believe the day has come when this class must finally create an organ worthy of representing it.

For lack of space, I cannot enter into detail here. So I shall limit my comments to giving the journal's title. For those who know how to grasp a whole order of ideas by a simple formula, this title and the epigraphs will suffice to make them understand perfectly the spirit in which I should like this journal to be edited.*

In order to give a very precise idea of the importance of the questions I propose to treat and of the order in which they would

SUNDAY

Through union, strength.   Brothers, let us unite.

THE WORKERS' UNION

HUMAN, SOCIAL, AND	RIGHT TO WORK.
POLITICAL UNITY.	RIGHT OF EDUCATION FOR
EQUALITY OF MEN AND WOMEN.	ALL MEN AND WOMEN.

JOURNAL OF THESE DUTIES AND INTERESTS

Wealth for all men and women.	Labor organization.
Equality, liberty, and justice for all.	Equitable compensation for work, talent, and capital.

One year, 12f; six months, 6f; three months, 3f.	Want ads, etc.

---

* In the first edition, the journal's title appeared only in the table of contents. In subsequent editions, a sample front page, as approximated here, was supplied. Tristan seems to contradict the sense of this paragraph by going ahead in the next passages with more detail about the contents of the proposed journal.

be placed, I am giving an analytical summary here of the subjects
to be found in each issue, with some variation:

1. *Of general interest* (that is to say, international, European,
government, and people's interests, the rich and the poor, etc.,
clearly demonstrating the tight solidarity existing between general and particular interests of nations, governments, classes and
individuals).

2. *On the rights and duties of governments and people*, the *rich* and
the *poor* (always in view of the common good).

3. *On religious, moral, and philosophical doctrines* (envisioned in
this triple relationship: what improvements can be made in the
people's mores, their material well-being, and their happiness?).

4. *On equal rights for men and women* (showing that there cannot
be any freedom, security, dignity, or happiness possible for man
as long as this equality is not recognized by law).

5. *Education* (proving that up to now mankind has not had any).

6. *Press review* (to spare the fatigue of reading all the news-
papers, and yet to keep the reader abreast of everything done and
said during the week domestically as well as abroad).

7. *Various news items* (bringing out useful information).

8. *Work, emigration and job lists, requests for work and for workers*
(everything important for the workers from all countries to know;
we have a special plan for this which will offer great opportunities
for workers and employers).

9. *Entertainment* (fables, tales, songs, plays, proverbs, anything
with a lesson).

Every month a column will tell of the remarkable works and
plays with a social aim. There will be reports on scientific, industrial, and other kinds of discoveries whose utility will be evident.

The financial part

Today in order to found a journal with any chance of success,
in my opinion, three indispensable conditions must be met: (1)

have an idea, a very determined goal, and have the moral, intellectual, and material interests of the majority of the nation revolve around this goal; (2) through the nobility of its aim, attract honest and courageous writers who are energetic enough to follow the path of progress, who can confront the most advanced questions on the social order, without being afraid to give clear and precise solutions to these questions; (3) acquire funds, not contributed by a single moneylender, but supplied by thousands cooperating in the work and each becoming through his small contribution an owner interested in the journal's success.

The Workers' Union would already possess the first two conditions, for it would have the *idea* and the *goal* and could easily find the right kind of writers. Only the third condition is missing: money, the indispensable fuel for all enterprises.

If the owners, petty bourgeois, and workers were well aware that it is in their own interest to have their existence as citizens finally represented, to have their fights as men finally discussed and demanded by serious, honest, and worthy writers, I do not doubt that each, understanding the work's importance, would hasten to help. And then the money needed to found a journal like this would be there in a few weeks. But, what a pity! Today's society, whether capitalist or proletarian, does not understand its true interests.

To attract as many stockholders as possible, I think a series of shares might be created and divided as follows: 500, 250, 100, 50, 25, 15, 10, and 5 francs. This way the price of the shares would be within reach for every pocketbook, the rich being able to buy at 500 and the poor for 5 francs. The shares will carry an interest of 4 percent and the dividend, depending upon profits, will be added to the revenue.

The cost of a subscription will be 15 francs a year. Workers in the same workshop or neighborhood will be able to group together in threes, fours, fives, and sixes to subscribe, thus entailing only a small expense for each.

I am proposing this idea of a journal without expecting its realization; yet one must never despair. What one cast aside yesterday and does not understand today, tomorrow perhaps one will accept and start to work on to realize a very simple thing, which for centuries might have been reputed to be utopian and impossible.

NOTE

1. Working men and women, salespeople, employees in certain offices, and many other types of laborers do not have time to read a daily paper. They need a journal appearing Saturday evening so they can read it on Sunday, Monday, and during the week at meal times.

SELECTIVE BIBLIOGRAPHY

WORKS BY FLORA TRISTAN

Nécessité de faire bon accueil aux femmes étrangères. Paris: Delaunay, 1835.

"Lettres à un architecte anglais." *Revue de Paris* (1837).

Pétition pour le rétablissement du divorce. Chambre des Députés, no. 133, Pét. 71 (December 20, 1837). Pamphlet in Archives nationales, Paris.

Pérégrinations d'une paria (1833–1834). Paris: A. Bertrand, 1838, 2 vols.

Méphis. Paris: Ladvocat, 1838.

"Pétition pour l'abolition de la peine de mort." *Journal du Peuple* (December, 1838). Pamphlet in Archives nationales, section moderne, Archives de la Chambre des Députés, Pét. 139, no. 70.

Promenades dans Londres. Paris: Raymond Bocquet, 1842.

Union ouvrière. Paris: Prévot, 1843.

"L'Emancipation de la femme ou le testament de la paria." Attributed to Tristan, published posthumously by A. Constant (1845).

Le Tour de France: Journal inédit 1843–1844. Preface by Michel Collinet, notes by Jules-L. Puech. Paris: Editions Tête de Feuilles, 1973.

BIOGRAPHIES OF TRISTAN

Baelen, Jean. *La Vie de Flora Tristan: socialisme et féminisme au XIXè siècle.* Paris: Seuil, 1972.

Blanc, Eléonore. *Biographie de Flora Tristan.* Lyon, 1845.

Desanti, Dominique. *A Woman in Revolt: A Biography of Flora*

Tristan. Translated by Elizabeth Zelvin. New York: Crown, 1976.

Gattey, Charles N. *Gauguin's Astonishing Grandmother: Biography of Flora Tristan.* London: Femina Books, 1970.

Puech, Jules-L. *La Vie et l'oeuvre de Flora Tristan, 1803–1844.* Paris: Marcel Rivière, 1925.

ARTICLES AND ESSAYS

Baelen, Jean. "Une Romantique oubliée: Flora Tristan." *Bulletin Guillaume Budé* (1970).

Breton, André. "Lettres inédites." *Le Surréalisme même* . . ., No. 4 (1954), pp. 4–12.

Goldsmith, Margaret, "Flora Tristan," in *Seven Women against the World.* London: Methuen & Co., 1935.

Gosset, Hélène. "Flora Tristan." *Maintenant*, Nos. 9–10 (1848), pp. 178–82.

Moon, S. Joan. "Feminism and Socialism: The Utopian Synthesis of Flora Tristan." In *Socialist Women: European Feminism in the Nineteenth and Twentieth Centuries,* edited by Marilyn Boxer and Jean Quataert. New York: Elsevier, 1978, pp. 19–50.

Ozouf, Mona. "La Fiancée de la révolution." *Le Nouvel Observateur*, 29 July 1978, p. 52. Review of the re-issue of *Promenades dans Londres.*

Rubel, Maximilien. "Flora Tristan et Karl Marx." *La Nef* (January, 1946), pp. 68–76.

Thibert, Marguerite. "Féminisme et socialisme d'après Flora Tristan." *Revue d'Histoire Economique et Sociale* (1921), pp. 115–36.

Zukerman, Phyllis. "Ideology and the Patriarchal Family: Nerval and Flora Tristan." *Sub-stance.* No. 15 (December, 1976), pp. 146–158.

INDEX

A NOTE ON THE TRANSLATOR

BEVERLY LIVINGSTON received her bachelor's degree from Northwestern University (1966) and her M.A. and Ph.D. from the University of Chicago (1969, 1974). She has taught at the University of Chicago and Yale University and was an Andrew Mellon Post-doctoral Fellow at the University of Pittsburgh. Among her publications are articles on the French "Nouveau Roman" in *Yale French Studies* and *The Romanic Review*.

The University of Illinois Press
is a founding member of the
Association of American University Presses.

University of Illinois Press
1325 South Oak Street
Champaign, IL 61820-6903
www.press.uillinois.edu